THE STUDY OF GREEK
INSCRIPTIONS

THE
STUDY OF GREEK
INSCRIPTIONS

BY

A. G. WOODHEAD

Fellow of Corpus Christi College and
Lecturer in Classics in the University of Cambridge

CAMBRIDGE
AT THE UNIVERSITY PRESS
1967

PUBLISHED BY
THE SYNDICS OF THE CAMBRIDGE UNIVERSITY PRESS

Bentley House, 200 Euston Road, London, N.W.1
American Branch: 32 East 57th Street, New York, N.Y. 10022

©

CAMBRIDGE UNIVERSITY PRESS
1959

First published 1959
Reprinted 1967
First paperback edition 1967

First printed in Great Britain at the University Press, Cambridge
Reprinted, by Lithography, in Great Britain by
Hazell Watson & Viney Ltd,
Aylesbury, Bucks

A·B·W ET A·G·W
PARENTIBVS CARISSIMIS
PIETATIS DOCVMENTVM

PREFACE

WHEN the writer of such a book as this first puts his pen to paper, or sets his first blank sheet in the typewriter, he is not at the beginning of his labours but approaching their end. While, on completing his task, he is indebted to those who have helped him and his manuscript with timely correction and criticism, he ought also to record his gratitude to those who over many years have encouraged his work and to whose support and inspiration he owes so much. That is why I welcome this opportunity of being able to express to Professors Sir Frank Adcock and Benjamin D. Meritt my sincere appreciation and affectionate regard for the many years in which I have enjoyed their advice and their friendship: to their guidance and encouragement I am conscious of a debt beyond my power to set down on paper, but which I am happy to acknowledge, inadequately though it be. Scholarly animosity is almost proverbial: it is particularly pleasant, therefore, to realise in one's own experience how intimately scholarship and friendship may be linked. For there are many others besides, whose regard and advice have been of the greatest value to me, not only in this present connexion but on many another occasion: in particular Professor W. den Boer, Dr Marcus N. Tod, and Mr A. M. Woodward, friends to whom I am grateful in a multitude of ways. Professors Jocelyn M. C. Toynbee, D. L. Page, Antony E. Raubitschek, and Homer A. Thompson, as well as Mr R. M. Cook, have read some or all of this work in the course of its development, and have given me much useful advice and salutary criticism; to them also I should like to express a warmth of appreciation which is personal as well as professional. Professor G. Klaffenbach's study *Griechische Epigraphik* appeared soon after my manuscript was complete; but it was not too late to take cognisance of a work which has to some extent the same scope as this, and my thanks are due to its author for his friendly assistance in this as in other matters. I must also acknowledge with thanks the permission of the Delegates of the Oxford University Press and the Council of the Society for the Promotion of Roman Studies to reproduce Plates 2 and 4 respectively.

Finally, since the greater part of this book was written in the course of a year spent at Princeton, New Jersey, while I was a member of the Institute for Advanced Study there, may I record my thanks to the Institute, its Director and staff, for the facilities which they so admirably provide and the welcome which they so warmly extend.

G. W.

Corpus Christi College, Cambridge
31 October 1957

CONTENTS

LIST OF ILLUSTRATIONS

FIGURES

PLATES

The numbers in the text refer to
the notes which begin on p. 120

INTRODUCTION

It is sometimes argued that, whereas classical studies retain in the modern world their value as an educational discipline in schools and universities, they have no real future at the level of research; all, it is said, that remains to be done is to dot the i's and cross the t's of the great Latinists and Hellenists who have gone before, or to resay in more modern terms what they have already said in a definitive form. Among the many possible arguments to the contrary, that provided by the study of Greek inscriptions is one of the most powerful. Chance and the trowel of the archaeologist have made and will continue to make available material for the study of antiquity hitherto unknown, in the light of which previous ideas must continually be restudied and reassessed. Epigraphy as a subject has developed to a striking degree in the last seventy-five years, both in the number of scholars who devote themselves to it and in the accuracy and intensity of their study of it; yet even so the material already at hand, to say nothing of what one may expect the fortunes of discovery and excavation in the future to produce, shows no signs of exhaustion in the contribution it can make to a better understanding of the ancient world. The humblest gravestone may have its value, and for that value to be properly realised it needs to be described and edited in careful detail. There is indeed no branch of classical studies which is unaffected by epigraphy. M. N. Tod, in his succinct but comprehensive survey of Greek epigraphy in the *Oxford Classical Dictionary*, remarked of Greek inscriptions that 'there is no aspect of Hellenic thought or speech, writing or action on which they do not throw valuable light'. Since all fields of classical studies are involved, the epigraphist must, in the first place, possess a sound general training in the classics as the point of departure for his more detailed work. But equally the specialist in any single field, or the student whose acquaintance with the major branches of classical studies is passing beyond the elementary, finds it increasingly necessary to know something of epigraphy, of the subject which continues to provide him with new data over which, otherwise, he would have no independent control.

It is to provide a brief route to such knowledge that this book has been written. There have been 'Introductions to Greek Epigraphy' in the past, of a more complex and detailed kind, and (since these are now out of date) there is room for more in the future. But such ambitious undertakings might tend rather to confuse than to assist the beginner, while for the scholar whose chief interests lie elsewhere the problem is not that of wanting an exhaustive survey, but of needing only to know where he stands, so that, without pretending to any specialised knowledge, he may at least feel he has the right to a judgement of his own. Such short surveys as exist[1] are limited in scope and perhaps not quite sufficient for the purpose suggested here. The resultant gap will, it is to be hoped, be in some measure filled by the chapters which follow, the usefulness of which will be measured not by the judgement of professional epigraphists, who will not need them and for whom they have not been written, but by that of the scholar or student for whom epigraphy ordinarily appears as some mystery practised by a comparatively narrow group of devotees. The work might indeed have been planned differently, and that it has many shortcomings will doubtless be pointed out with alacrity. For example, since Greek epigraphy concerns all branches of Greek activity, there is room for a study which will take each branch separately and analyse, with examples, the sort of contribution which epigraphy has made to it. This book has been written with the historian in mind, and in particular with a view to the needs of the student of Athenian history, which looms the largest in the ordinary curriculum. But, *mutatis mutandis*, what has been set down here can prove of no less value to those in other fields, who should not be deterred, simply because many of the problems mentioned are historical and the examples quoted Attic, into thinking that the lessons of it do not apply to them.

It would, of course, be well to begin with a definition of what Greek epigraphy is, but this has been so concisely put by M. N. Tod that it is necessary only to quote what he has said.[2] It is perhaps rather more opportune to emphasise one or two fundamental points about the study, and in particular to ask ourselves what is the province of the epigraphist, on the one hand, and of the historian or the scholar in any of the fields which epigraphy may be said to 'serve', on the other. This question has provoked a good deal of discussion in recent years and has led to the championship of two diametrically opposed points of view.[3] To one school of thought epigraphy is an 'ancillary' study, the fruits of which come to reinforce what is the primary or great subject of classical research, the study of the literary texts. On this view, the epigraphist's duty is that of establishing the most probable text of an inscription, and no more. The work of its integration into the general body of 'received knowledge' will be that of the historian or philosopher or expert in whatever field is involved. On the other side it is maintained that the epigraphist's primary duty is to interpret his inscription, and that he only is properly qualified for the work of integration—indeed that it is to him that history must look for its future writing. The truth perhaps lies, as usually, somewhere between the extremes. Epigraphy is, as has been described, too vital and important a subject for it to be depressed into a subordinate position; nor is the epigraphist, tenacious of the text on which he has laboured, likely to surrender it readily for the interpretative work on it to be done elsewhere. But, on the other hand, inscriptions with which the epigraphist may be faced may cover a wide span both of time and space—a millennium of history and an area from Britain to Pakistan, with a corresponding variety of subject-matter, and he cannot pretend to such an *expertise* as will allow him, except for a restricted area or a limited subject, to speak with authority. With specialisation, not only in epigraphy but also in other necessary and contributory subjects, at such a high level and with such a growing exclusiveness, the task of the historian becomes much more like that of a supreme commander in the field, who marshals the efforts of all the components of his forces but who, himself, has no intimate and expert knowledge of the detail of each component. The study of the texts takes its place beside epigraphy as a component part of the material of history. But just as any classical scholar, when he comes to a *crux* in his text, has at least some knowledge of what the problem is and how it is to be solved, by reading his *apparatus criticus*, so must he be able to approach the epigraphic contribution to his studies with sufficient knowledge for his immediate purpose. And the epigraphist, while not undertaking to do the historian's work for him, must go far enough beyond the simple establishment of the text, and suggest, with reference to the major sources, modern as well as ancient, enough of an interpretation for the historian to find the general lines along which advance is possible laid down for him.

One of the principal features about the study of Greek inscriptions is the closeness of contact which they give us with the ancient world. This has been remarked upon often enough, but the vividness never loses its magic and its appeal. That in some weather-beaten fragment we have, before our eyes, the very words of an important and perhaps, in the event, world-shaking decision as inscribed soon after the decision was taken, that we are so to speak reaching across more than two thousand years and grasping the stone-cutter's hand after he had finished writing words perhaps vital to the future of civilisation as we know it, remains perpetually and profoundly moving, and can hardly fail to stir the imagination of even the most stolid student of the classics. Of the closeness of this contact, and of the light it throws into places otherwise dark, more will be said in subsequent chapters. But that epigraphy is a *compelling* subject cannot be too strongly emphasised, and the enthusiasm of those who study it bears witness to the strength of its appeal to the imaginative as well as to the dryly rational aspects of the scholar's mind.

It is sometimes claimed for inscriptions that they provide not only a vivid but also an objective witness of the events with which they are related, that whereas a literary author writes with his own ideas and interpretation as a basis, an inscription is an official record, whose objectivity can do much to redress the balance of the ancient historian's subjective account. But this objectivity has been much overstressed and misinterpreted, and a record which is committed to stone does not on that account derive some additional and indisputable veracity. Few people who read the eulogies on gravestones of a century or two ago would be prepared to believe all the superlatives that they see there. The existence of a decree to take certain action may not mean that the action was in fact taken or, if it was taken, that it was either successful or important. An 'honorary decree' may have been drafted while the proposer's tongue was in his cheek; it is no final proof of the merits of the person honoured. Inscriptions cannot therefore be unhesitatingly assumed to say what they mean or to mean what they say. As with a modern communiqué, there is sometimes more reading to be done between the lines than on them, and the art of propaganda, though brought to its finest pitch by modern techniques, was not absent from the armoury of the politician of antiquity. Objectivity can therefore not be assumed; but we have the consolation of knowing that we are reading what it was intended at the time should be read, and our contact with the occasion itself remains immediate and important.

That the chances of survival through so many centuries, and the mutilated condition of so many of the texts that have survived, make the material and the results of epigraphic studies so fragmentary and partial needs no emphasis. It is only here and there that epigraphy can throw its shafts of light. These shafts are sometimes intense, more frequently pale and faltering. More often than not, the acquisition of new epigraphic evidence on a problem serves only to put more questions than it resolves. But the striking contributions that epigraphy has made to classical studies sometimes lead to an over-emphasis of its possibilities of which it is advisable to beware. Even if many more inscriptions survived, and even if all the surviving inscriptions were intact and unmutilated, the epigraphist would not be in possession of all the answers to the problems he would like to solve. Nor ought we to allow our own preoccupation with what epigraphy can contribute to cause us to overestimate the importance of the material it does contribute. The restoration of the great decree and assessment list by which, in 425 B.C., a higher rate of tribute was imposed on the Athenian allies is one of the triumphs of modern epigraphy,[4] and now forms an important feature of any discussion of the Archidamian War. But Thucydides makes no reference to it in his *History*. He may well have had reasons, and good ones, for not doing so, and he should not be condemned, as he has been, for not knowing his own business best. Such a tendency to insist that Thucydides writes his history on our terms is perhaps symptomatic of a disposition to overvalue the new and exciting testimony which inscriptions provide, and this could lead to errors no less than would a total ignorance of the epigraphic contribution.

With these warnings in mind let the reader go on to explore for himself the richness of material which the study of inscriptions offers him—material which is not confined to the smooth and regular stelae which bore the official documents of the city-state, but which will include objects of bronze and terracotta, casual and ill-formed graffiti, and a variety of household articles which, for one reason or another, carried some written sign or message. The epigraphist's field is wide, and the contribution he can make comes no less by the patient accumulation of details from here and there, or the collection of statistical data from a large number of texts, than from the discovery and edition of some single document of primary and fundamental importance. If this book, as a vade-mecum in the hands of the non-specialist, can lead to a wider appreciation and understanding of the problems of epigraphy and of its future value for the development of classical studies, it will have done all that is required of it.

CHAPTER I

SIGNS AND SYMBOLS

THE editor of an epigraphic text is faced at the outset by the problem of conveying to his readers a general picture of the inscription with which he is dealing—how much of the original stone still survives and is legible, what he can see of the parts not easily legible, his ideas if any on the extent and contents of the sections now lost. The reader cannot turn to the stone and see for himself what is there and what is not, nor, even if he could, would the editor's own contributions be made clear to him thereby. It is, as a result, necessary to use a number of conventional signs, which present no difficulties to the printer and which help to explain in an easily recognisable way the restorations and corrections which the new edition offers, along with a readable text of the inscription as it stands.

It is not often that inscribed stones survive to us complete, or that what does survive is completely and readily legible. If a stone has been broken, fractions of letters at the point of breakage may provide disputed readings, or it may be that the stone has been re-used as a threshold block or something similar, so that the lettering has been worn practically smooth by the tread of many feet, making the exact text to be read uncertain. Possibly part of the lettering was at some time purposely chiselled away; or the editor may believe that the workman who inscribed the stone made an error in the process of his work, through inattention or misunderstanding of the draft he was copying. Or, if a word is written on the stone in an abbreviated form, it may be necessary for the readers' comfort to show what the editor understands the complete form to have been. For all these purposes certain commonly agreed symbols are in use, and they form a necessary part of the epigraphist's stock-in-trade.

In the past there was a good deal of variety in the details of these usages. In 1931 the International Congress of Orientalists at Leiden agreed upon a uniform system applicable both to papyri and inscriptions, and this system, generally known as the Leiden system, has since then been adopted by most scholars working in these subjects.[1] But objectors still remain, and idiosyncrasies persist,[2] so that it is advisable, before using an epigraphic work, whether it be pre- or post-1931, to consult the section on 'Sigla' at the beginning to make sure what the writer intends by the signs he employs.[3]

Texts may be written either continuously, like the text in a book, or with a division of lines corresponding to those on the stone itself. The former system[4] saves space and paper, but is sometimes confusing and tedious to read, and gives no clear impression of the actual aspect of the stone, with the result that the epigraphic problems can be far less readily appreciated. When such a method is used, it is customary to insert an upright line in the text to indicate where a new line begins on the stone, and to insert a double upright line (‖) to mark the beginning of every fifth line on the stone. These latter are usually accompanied by a figure (5, 10, 15, etc.) in the margin, for ease of reference. French epigraphists seem to prefer a marginal notation of fours rather than of fives,[5] but the principle remains the same. As an example, lines 2 and following of *IG* II² 337 (M. N. Tod, *GHI* II 189),[6] when printed in a continuous text on this method, appear as

    Ἐπὶ Νικοκράτους ἄρχοντ|ος, ἐπὶ τῆς Αἰγεῖδος πρώτ|ης πρυτα-
5 νείας· τῶν προέδ‖ρων ἐπεψήφιζεν Θεόφιλο|ς Φηγούσιος· ἔδοξεν
    τῆι β|ουλεῖ, κτλ.

But if the lines be printed as they actually appear on the stone, the text will be

            Ἐπὶ Νικοκράτους ἄρχοντ
            ος, ἐπὶ τῆς Αἰγεῖδος πρώτ
            ης πρυτανείας· τῶν προέδ
5   ρων ἐπεψήφιζεν Θεόφιλο
            ς Φηγούσιος· ἔδοξεν τῆι β
            ουλεῖ, κτλ.

With this second method, it is at once clear to the eye that the text in question is narrow, with few letters in each line, and the shape of the printing to some extent is able to reflect the shape of the inscription itself. If space allows, it is therefore the method greatly to be preferred, and is in fact that generally used in the larger works of reference, as well as in the periodicals and detailed works in which the primary publications of inscriptions are made, or in which older editions are discussed and revised.

Among the primary weapons in the epigraphist's typographic armament are brackets of various shapes, which it is necessary to describe in detail. Square brackets [ ] are used to enclose letters printed in his text which the editor believes to have originally stood on the stone, but which are now totally illegible or totally lost. For example, at the end of *IG* I² 118 (M. N. Tod, *GHI* I² 90), an Athenian decree of 408/7 B.C.

in honour of Oeniades of Sciathus (Plate 2), the text of lines 27 and
following may be printed as   ἐς δ

[ἐ τ]ὴν γνώμην μεταγράψαι ἀντ
[ὶ τõ Σ]κιαθίο ὅπως ἂν ἦι γεγρα
30   [μμένο]ν Οἰνιάδην τὸν Παλαισ
[κιάθιον].

It will be clear from the photograph that the stone is broken away at
the bottom left-hand corner, and the letters enclosed by the square
brackets are no longer to be seen. But the editors have believed that,
when the stone was intact, those letters stood there, and they indicate
as much by including them in the text, but with the brackets to distinguish them as editorial supposition rather than actual fact.

Round brackets ( ) enclose letters added by the editor to complete a
word expressed on the stone in an abbreviated form. Such abbreviations occur particularly frequently with names of demes, with Latin
praenomina, and with familiar words such as Θεός in Christian inscriptions. The editor may thus, for clarity, write Γαρ(γήττιος) for what
appears on the stone as Γαρ, or Πό(πλιος) for Πό, or Θ(εό)ς for Θ̄Σ̄
(abbreviations are sometimes indicated on the stone itself by a horizontal line above the shortened word). But he may prefer to print the
abbreviations as they stand. Compare, for instance, *SEG* XII 120,
XIII 469, XIV 92 and 97.

Angled brackets ⟨ ⟩ serve two purposes. They enclose letters which
the engraver of the stone accidentally left out, or they enclose correct
letters inserted by the editor to replace wrong ones written on the stone.
The editor usually notes the reading of the stone itself in explanation of
his use of this sign. For example, in *SEG* XII 371, a stone from Cos recording a Messenian decree regarding the Coan sanctuary of Asclepius,
a phrase in lines 13–14 refers to τῶν ἐμ Μεσσάναι κατο⟨ι⟩κε[ύν]‖των. The
square brackets show, as described earlier, that the two letters at the
end of line 13 are missing, the stone being broken at that point. What the
stone actually shows at the end of line 13 is ΤΩΝΕΜΜΕΣΣΑΝΑΙΚΑΤΟΚΕ.
The accidentally omitted *iota* has been supplied by the editor in his
text as ⟨ι⟩. In the same inscription the word θεαρός is divided between
lines 22 and 23. The last two letters of line 22 are lost, and of the first
half of the word only *theta* survives: at the beginning of line 23 the
engraver, perhaps letting his mind wander for a moment, wrote ΡΩΣ
for ΡΟΣ. The printed text of this word may therefore be set down as
θ[εα]‖ρ⟨ό⟩ς.

Hooked brackets { } are only used when the engraver has put in too many letters or has mistakenly repeated letters or words. In the same *SEG* XII 371 this occurs twice in three lines (10–12). In line 10 the stone-cutter has written ἐμάνυον τὰν τὰν εὔνοια[ν], mistakenly repeating the definite article, which in the printed text will appear as τὰν {τὰν}. Similarly, καί at the end of line 11 was written again at the beginning of line 12, the writer having forgotten that he had included it in the previous line: as a result, on its second appearance it is printed as {καί}.

Errors were sometimes noticed by the stone-cutter himself, and he made efforts to erase them. Or it may be that a *rasura* was deliberately made on a correctly engraved inscription by reason of changed official policy, *damnatio memoriae*, or the like. Typical examples are *SEG* XII 515–17, one an honorary altar and the other two milestones of the third century A.D. from Cilicia. The letters thought to have been present in the parts of the stone which were erased are enclosed in double square brackets ⟦ ⟧. In these cases the Emperors Macrinus, Severus Alexander, and their relatives suffered *damnatio memoriae* after their deaths, and their names were officially expunged from the records. In line 3 of *SEG* XII 516 all that now appears on the stone between M. and Σεουήρῳ is a rough blank space, lower in level than the original surface of the stone surrounding it. It is clear that the name Ὀπελλίῳ once filled the space, and this may, as a result, be printed as ⟦Ὀπελλίῳ⟧.

It frequently happens on inscriptions that, where the stone is broken away, some part of a letter may be seen at the edge of the break, without it being clear what the letter was. Suppose, for instance, the edge shows the upper part of an angled letter, Λ. This might have been Α, Δ, or Λ. It may be clear in the context which of the three it in fact was: if we suppose it was an *alpha*, the editor would be entitled to print it outside the square brackets, since it is not pure restoration on his part, but he would set a dot beneath it (α̣) to show that the letter is incomplete, and that such traces as remain of it agree with his interpretation. In Plate 2, the decree about Oeniades of Sciathus referred to above, the letters near the break at the foot of the stone are partly destroyed. But parts of *eta* at the beginning of line 28 and of *kappa* at the beginning of line 29 are discernible, and we may therefore write in the text τ]ὴγ and Σ]κιαθίο. In line 30 the right-hand tip of the final *nu* of γεγραμμένο]ν is also visible. Any imperfect letter should be distinguished by its dot, even if its identity can be regarded as to all intents and purposes certain.[7]

Dots on, not below, the line are used to show where missing letters are presumed to have stood, in cases where the editor suggests no restoration. Each dot represents one missing letter, and this device is generally used when the extent of the lacuna can be accurately judged. In *IG* I² 26 (*SEG* XIII 3), an Athenian treaty with the Delphic Amphictiony of *c.* 458 B.C., the text of line 2 is printed as [οι,...ντὶς ἐπρ]-υτάνευε κτλ. There are firm grounds for certainty that the name of the tribe in prytany consisted of no more nor less than seven letters, but since this leaves the tribes Aiantis and Leontis as equal possibilities, no definite restoration can be offered: the ΝΤΙΣ at the end of the name is sure in either case, but in front of it three dots are printed to indicate the space available.

Where it is uncertain how many letters are missing, dashes (- - - -) are used instead of dots, the number of dashes having no reference even to the possible or likely number of missing letters: but, as with the dots, an approximate number is sometimes printed above the dashes as a guide, e.g. _ _ _^{c. 15} _ _. Compare for example *IG* I² 60 (*SEG* XIII 8), a treaty between Athens and Mytilene of the Archidamian War period, where in line 2 the heading reads [_ _⁶_ _ ἐγραμμάτ]ευε.

If the stone-cutter has left blank a space which, in a continuous text, would have been expected to contain a letter, this is indicated in the printed version by an italic *v* (or in *SEG* an underlined v̲). Each *v* equals one blank letter space, so that *vvv* will represent four blank spaces, *vvvv* five, and so on. To indicate that the whole of the remainder of a line, or the whole space below an inscribed line, is devoid of lettering, the complete word *vacat* or its abbreviation *vac.* may be inserted. In Plate 2, the stele is blank below the last inscribed line, and line 31 is blank on the surviving part of the stone, although it is clear that the text extended into that line in the section now lost. To show that both the remainder of line 31, and also everything below it, remain uninscribed, it would be reasonable to print this last part of the text as

[κιάθιον]. *vac.*
vacat

These symbols, when they are properly understood and taken note of, guide the reader in seeing, through the editor's eyes, what the stone shows and may be presumed to have shown, and what the editor thinks about it. It must be remembered (and this is all too often forgotten) that what is within the square brackets does not exist save in the editor's opinion, however well founded that opinion may be, and there is no accepted way of distinguishing a sound restoration from a hazardous one.[8] The editor will presumably give in his commentary the reasons which have led him to insert the restorations he prints, and it is for the reader himself to deliberate on their validity. He may conclude that they are justly made and that they may fairly be used as evidence; but he is entitled to the opposite conclusion if he prefers it.

Even so, much will remain printed in the text, set down on the basis of the editor's observation and research, which the reader, lacking opportunity or leisure to retrace the whole ground to his own satisfaction, will have to take on trust. He cannot check everything which the editor tells him. A good photograph will give him some chance to control the published readings with reference to the stone, and most publications now include a good picture or indicate where one may be found. But all the same it is wise to exercise caution in the use of restored texts. It happens remarkably often that the vital part of an inscription is the part which has not survived, and scholarly discussion is constantly finding cause for argument in epigraphic restorations, as well as the means to improve them. The signs and symbols must therefore not only be recognised but must be scrupulously observed, and a familiarity with them is essential to any further and closer use of epigraphic material. That is why it has been desirable, and wellnigh essential, to devote Chapter I to them.

CHAPTER II

THE ORIGIN AND DEVELOPMENT OF THE GREEK ALPHABET

THIS book is concerned only with Greek written in the characters familiar to us and used by the Greeks themselves, with changes only of detail, from the archaic period to the present time. That is to say, it excludes the written records of the Mycenaean period in Greece and of the Minoan civilisation in Crete, although these have been interpreted as written in an early form of the Greek language, antedating Homer by half-a-dozen centuries and yet with features recognisably akin in many instances to Homeric Greek. The decipherment of the Minoan–Mycenaean writing by Michael Ventris has won a general acceptance as providing evidence of the earliest written Greek known to us,[1] and to that extent it may be said that it requires to be included under the general head of Greek epigraphy. But it is so obviously a subject *sui generis*, and tolerably self-contained, that it is better to preserve it as a separate study and not include it here. The art of writing at that period was probably not widespread:[2] but after the fall of the Mycenaean kingdoms it was, as it seems, totally lost. The famous reference in Homer (*Iliad* VI, 168) to σήματα λυγρά sounds very much as a memory of bygone literacy echoed by one to whom writing was unfamiliar and mysterious. At any rate, so far as the evidence goes, it was at least three centuries after the fall of Mycenae before literacy was re-established, and then the form in which the language was expressed was completely different. Except in the case of the syllabary used by the Cypriotes, which also lies outside the present scope, no continuity in the method of writing Greek is discernible between the Mycenaean and archaic periods. Nor was the new method a native product of Greece itself. The Greeks' own tradition was that they imported their classical alphabet from Phoenicia, and ascribed it to Cadmus. The Cadmean connexion may result from a confusion with traditions of the early writing we now identify as Mycenaean, but a Phoenician origin for the Greek alphabet as we know it is sure.[3] Not only does the universal voice of ancient tradition name Phoenicia, but a comparison of the earliest Greek alphabets with those current along the Syrian coast shows that they share four important elements, all of which help to confirm the connexion.

(1) The forms of the letters are remarkably akin, and the closeness of

their resemblance has been used as an argument in the discussion of the date at which the Greeks adopted the Phoenician alphabet, a matter more fully considered below. (2) The names of the letters in Greek resemble the corresponding Phoenician names. But whereas *alpha*, *beta*, *gamma*, etc., are no more than labels, and are meaningless in themselves, the Phoenician *aleph*, *beth*, *gimel*, etc., all have a meaning— *aleph* 'ox', *beth* 'house', and so forth. The Greek versions are no more than mnemonics, with the merit that the first letter of each word makes the sound of the letter of the alphabet which the word represents. (3) The values of the Phoenician letters are, with the exception of the vowels (discussed later), more or less those reproduced by the Greeks. (4) Finally, the earliest Greek writing adopted the same direction as that of the Phoenician, from right to left, or, as it appears to us, backwards. This evidence, briefly stated though it is, bears out the view of the ancients themselves. The major questions concerning the early Greek alphabet are not, therefore, where the Greeks found it, which is abundantly clear, but when they took it over, and, taking into account the modifications they made in it, how it was disseminated through the Greek world.

The date at which this 'take-over' occurred has been much debated.[4] The traditional connexion with Cadmus and other figures of mythology would put it back to heroic times, and until the last generation such a dating was generally accepted. However, there is no actual inscriptional evidence from Greece which antedates the eighth century, and very little which can be safely attributed even as early as that. An *argumentum ex silentio* may not, under ordinary circumstances, be a very powerful argument, but in this case the *silentium* is so complete that it is hard to press counter-arguments—for example that earlier documents existed but have perished; this would be simply to explain *ignotum per ignotius*. The literacy of the so-called 'Dark Ages' would have to be proved by further discoveries, especially in view of the complete break between the Mycenaean and classical Greek scripts. The view of Rhys Carpenter, that the 'take-over' occurred only a little earlier than the earliest epigraphic texts which survive to us, has won increasing acceptance among scholars as not going beyond the limits of the available evidence.

But there are more positive grounds for accepting a date for the adoption of the Greek alphabet in the early eighth century. There is, for instance, the 'criterion of close approach'. Since the Greek script is admittedly Phoenician in origin, and since its letters resemble those of the Phoenician coast, it seems reasonable to look to a time when that resemblance was at its closest, and when the forms of the earliest Greek letters have some close counterpart in Phoenician epigraphy. This criterion has been that around which much of the controversy provoked by Carpenter's thesis has revolved, and it remains true, as was long ago noted, that the resemblance between early Greek letter-forms and those on the so-called Moabite or Mesha stone (of the early ninth century) is particularly close. Earlier than that, Phoenician characters have less resemblance to those of the earliest Greek. Later, the two again diverge, and there are wide differences between Greek and Phoenician, for example, in the sixth and later centuries. It is also noteworthy that particularly in the eighth century Greek contacts with the Orient were again in a flourishing state, after a lapse which followed the end of the Mycenaean period, and Greek trade with the eastern Mediterranean was, on the evidence of archaeology, fully and profitably established. Oriental artistic motifs began to affect and to transform the accepted Greek patterns of ornamentation, and the change of style from the Geometric to the Orientalising seems to coincide in date with the increase in Greco-oriental trade relations and with the period at which Greek written records, as we know them, begin. It appears plausible, as a result, that in the ninth–eighth centuries these contacts with Phoenicia were the occasion for the transmission not only of artistic but also of alphabetic ideas, and that the Greeks learned their letters from those orientals with whom their contacts were most direct.

It was probably through the intercourse of trade, especially in such depots as Al-Mina (Posideion), that the usefulness of literacy impressed itself on the Greek merchants. These, perhaps each for himself, acquired some local alphabetic version suitable to their own use, which they would take home with them.[5] The other citizens, on their return, recognised the usefulness of this new means of communication and record, and adopted it for themselves. There was, however, no uniformity save in general terms. The transmission was haphazard, and the alphabetic pattern of archaic Greece, as it gradually begins to emerge, shows a general confusion. The alphabets of each city and region, while corresponding in many essentials, show wide and characteristic divergences in others. In the archaic period it is thus readily possible in most cases to distinguish the inscriptions of one city or area from those of another simply by studying the forms of the letters used. The alphabetic history of the next centuries is one of the gradual ironing out of these distinctions, and of the progressive adoption by the whole Greek world of the version of the alphabet originally used by the East Greeks of the coast of Asia Minor, the Ionic alphabet.

In the course of the transmission and general adoption of the Phoenician letters, certain significant modifications were made by the Greeks, which it is essential to understand. In the first place, they introduced the vowels. Vowels were not expressed in Phoenician writing, although it is possible that the letters *aleph, he, yod* and *ayin* were beginning to acquire some vocalic character. It is at least probable that, when spoken, they sounded like vowels to Greek ears. At all events, these four letters (A, E, I and O) appear in Greek from the very outset in full use as vowels, while an extra one was added at the end of the alphabet, unknown to the Phoenicians but common to all the Greeks, *upsilon*. Secondly, the Phoenicians were rich in sibilants, richer indeed than was necessary for the Greeks. Some of these letters were rejected as otiose, and others were confused in the course of transmission, so that the resultant pattern is somewhat complex. *Sigma* was formed by tilting the original Phoenician *shin* either 90 degrees (ξ, ʒ) or a full half circle (M), but in this latter form it was known by the name of another Phoenician sibilant, *tsade*, and called *san* in Greek by those who used it.[6] *San* is not found where *sigma* exists, and *vice versa*, but it is remarkable that both are included in specimen copies of the alphabet, written out as exercises or reminders, which have survived from the early period. The Phoenician *samekh* was dropped in some areas, where it was replaced by the letter χ or a makeshift *chi* plus *sigma*; but even where it was retained its name seems to have been transmuted or forgotten, and the name *xi* is a vocalised letter of the same kind of invention as *phi, chi* and *psi*.

∝	A
β	ᴎ - B
γ	ᒣ - Γ
δ	Δ
ε	Ϝ - E
ʒ	I?
ʻhʼ	H
θ	⊙
ι	ᒣ - I
κ	K
λ	ᒣ - ∧
μ	ᴍ - M
ν	N - N
ο	C
π	Γ
san	M
ϱ	Ɒ - P
τ	T
υ	V Y
ω	O
Φ = ΓH , X = KH	
Ψ = ΓM , Ξ = KM	

Fig. 1. The epichoric alphabet of Melos, with its Ionic equivalent.

NOTE. *San* was gradually replaced by *sigma*. *Koppa* is not attested in the surviving inscriptions, but may be presumed to have existed. Ψ on several gravestones has been held to equal ξ.

The invention of these last three letters draws attention to the fact that, to different degrees in different places, the Greeks found that the Phoenician alphabet in the form in which it had come to them was inadequate to provide all the sounds that they wished to express. Three extra letters Φ, X and Ψ, the 'additional' letters, as they are customarily called, were added to the alphabet by the large majority of the Greeks. *Phi*, where it was adopted, was everywhere given the same value of an aspirated *p*, but the values assigned to what we know as *chi* and *psi* were not universally the same. The variety in their use in fact divides the Greek world alphabetically into two parts, and this geographic division based on the additional letters has been found in the past of basic importance for the study and classification of the Greek alphabets. In most of mainland Greece the sign X represented *x* or *k+s*, while Ψ stood for *k+h*, or an aspirated *k*. Alphabets showing this use of the additional letters are classed as of the 'western' group. East Greece, on the other hand, together with some cities around the isthmus of Corinth, used the two letters in the way familiar to us, X for *chi* and Ψ for *p+s* or *psi*; these areas also retained the Phoenician *samekh* for *k+s*, a letter dropped by the western group. The type of alphabet as used by this second group is classed as 'eastern'. Attica, with an eastern alphabet in respect to *chi*, did not use either *xi* or *psi*. But a further group, sometimes known as the 'primitive' group, stood apart from these two major divisions. The islands of Crete, Thera and Melos in the southern Aegean area, from the first two of which early inscriptional evidence is forthcoming, did not at first admit the three additional letters at all, but expressed these mixed sounds in full as ΓH, KH, ΓM and KM (these alphabets being *san*- and not *sigma*-users).[7]

Although this geographical division on the basis of the additional letters is convenient, and appears in the handbooks as the basic distinction to be observed, too great a stress should not be laid on it. A survey of the other letters, which were more directly taken over from the Phoenicians, produces different geographic patterns. But since it is so frequently mentioned it is as well to be fully conversant with it, and its terminology is useful for easy reference.

The need to distinguish in writing between long and short *o* was not widely felt in the Greek world during the early period, but attempts were made in one or two places in the Aegean to show the difference. It was on the Asiatic coast that the means of differentiation was achieved which in the end commended itself to the universal acceptance of the Greeks. A new letter, Ω, was tacked on to the end of the alphabet, after the additional letters already discussed, and this was held to represent the long *o* sound. The already existing O thus became restricted in use to the short vowel. Very early inscriptions from Ionia are few. The earliest so far discovered is the 'graffito of Dolion',[8] of the seventh century, and this shows *omega* as already in existence. But its variable use in later Ionic inscriptions, notably some of the graffiti from

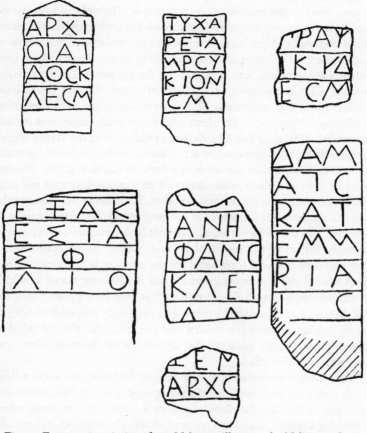

Fig. 2. Funerary inscriptions from Melos, to illustrate the Melian epichoric alphabet. Drawings based on *IG* XII 3, 1130–1180.

Abu Simbel of the first decade of the sixth century,[9] and in dedications made at Naucratis, suggests that in the early sixth century it was still something of a novelty. Speculation as to the place and method of its invention is hardly profitable, but it may have been created on the analogy of *eta* (see below). Nor is it clear why the separate expression of long *o* (and of long *e*) should have been felt as desirable only, in the first place, in certain restricted areas of Greece: the remainder of the Greeks apparently adopted it as convenient rather than necessary, and the growth of its popularity is traceable in the surviving inscriptions of the archaic period.

The letter H represented, in most parts of the Greek world including Athens, the 'rough breathing' or aspirate *h*. In Ionia, however, the same letter was used, not as an *h*, but as a long *e*, distinguishing it from *epsilon* or short *e*. Here no new letter had to be invented and added to the alphabet, for it happened that one of the letters already taken over from the Phoenicians was available for the purpose. The Ionians, in common with the peoples of Elis and of Crete, did not express the rough breathing or aspirate at all, but were, according to the technical terminology, 'psilotic'. To them the Phoenician letter *heth* would become *eth*. Since, as has already been pointed out, the Greek names for the letters of the alphabet are acrophonic, the first letter of the name expressing the sound of the letter to which the name is given, Phoenician *heth* provided the Ionians not with an aspirate but with the suggestion of another *e* sound additional to Phoenician *he*, *epsilon*: the available letter was in fact used for the long sound, restricting *epsilon* to the short, and this differentiation, like that between *omicron* and *omega*, gradually spread to the rest of the Greek world. Some confusion of these two uses of H, for long *e* and for the aspirate, is visible in various places during the transitional period, and inscriptions occur in which the same letter is used for both duties.[10] It may be suggested that the availability of an additional letter *e* was originally responsible for the Ionian distinction between *epsilon* and *eta*, and that the 'need' thus created produced by analogy the differentiation between long and short *o* already discussed.

It has been mentioned that the period between the seventh and fourth centuries witnessed the gradual spread of the Ionic usages, and the supersession by the Ionic alphabet of the various local, often termed 'epichoric', alphabets up and down Greece. At Athens the change was made for official documents by a decree proposed by Archinus in the archonship of Euclides (403/2 B.C.), after which these were without exception written in Ionic letters. Earlier in the fifth century Ionic usages had occasionally intruded into official as well as private inscriptions, and towards the end of the century whole documents were sometimes written in Ionic characters even though that alphabet was not officially prescribed. This occurs during the Archidamian War, and with some frequency in the period of the restored democracy between 410 and 404. Thus it cannot be assumed as a kind of axiom that any Athenian document expressed in Ionic letters necessarily postdates 403/2.[11]

No such fixed date for the adoption of the Ionic alphabet exists in the case of other cities or areas, but in the surviving inscriptions the gradual intrusion of the Ionic forms can be recognisably followed. In dealing with the epichoric inscriptions of a given area it is possible to suggest, with some degree of accuracy, a useful relative chronology based not only on the development of the letter-forms there used, as noted earlier, but also on the amount of 'Ionic intrusion' which has taken place. An epichoric inscription using an *eta*, when others from the same place use *epsilon* for long *e*, is likely to be later in date than they, and this may be borne out by the fact that the individual letters are better formed, or more akin in shape to the canonical types of the classical period. The same is true of the use of Ψ for *p+s*, in places where it has hitherto represented *k+h*, or the use of the same letter in a city such as Athens where *p+s* was previously represented by ΦΣ. Indeed it is true to say that dating by these means sometimes leads to a more precise chronology than is possible once the whole process of alphabetic development has been completed and the epichoric alphabets have passed out of use.[12]

The comparative study of the epichoric alphabets, and of the extent to which they were affected by the Ionic usages, is made easier by such collections of facsimiles as H. Roehl's *Imagines Inscriptionum Antiquissimarum* (ed. 3, 1907).[13] As an example, Fig. 2 shows a selection of tombstones from the island of Melos, a member of Kirchhoff's southern, primitive, or 'green' group, which may be dated in the sixth and fifth centuries. They are not here arranged in chronological order, but it is not difficult to sort them into it according both to the development of the shapes of the letters and to the degree of 'Ionicism'. It also affords an illustration of the Melian alphabet, known best in its earlier form from the so-called 'Colonna Naniana', of the middle of the sixth century, from which most of the letter-forms shown in Fig. 1 are copied.[14] The 'crooked' *iota* had already given way to the straight form before the tombstone series begins, by which time also the use of *chi* had become established. Melos, it may be noted, was one centre at which an attempt to distinguish the two lengths of the *o* sound was made, but the method there favoured never achieved a more than local currency.

The standard handbooks of Greek epigraphy, such as W. Larfeld's *Griechische Epigraphik* or E. S. Roberts' *Introduction to Greek Epigraphy*, provide tables of the Greek epichoric alphabets as they existed at different periods of their development, and the reader may be referred to these for fuller information. However, Larfeld's book is more than forty, and Roberts' now seventy, years old, and in many cases newer evidence has become available to make modifications and improvements to our knowledge. The best and most up-to-date work of reference is now L. H. Jeffery's *The Local Scripts of Archaic Greece*, a study devoted exclusively to Greek inscriptions of the early period, and the epichoric forms are there discussed with a more comprehensive and accurate description of their character and development than was possible in an earlier generation. It is wise to note, in the case of the older works on the subject, that printed type, or a printer's 'epigraphic fount', does not always do justice to the exact forms of the individual letters, which may vary not only from one inscription to another but even within the same inscription. It is advisable, therefore, to check these lists with photographs or drawings whenever accuracy is required, and the same advice is valid also for the printed reproductions of epichoric inscriptions which sometimes have to suffice, in the textbooks, for a facsimile drawing. It is only from accurate reproduction that the epichoric forms can be properly studied and appreciated.

Apart from the alphabets of Ionia and Attica, that most likely to be met with in the ordinary course of events is the epichoric alphabet of Corinth. Few stone-cut inscriptions of early date survive from Corinth itself or its immediate neighbourhood. The destruction carried out by L. Mummius in 146 B.C. no doubt robbed us of much possible material. More destructive may have been the robbing of stone from the empty and decaying site. There are, however, some interesting monuments of the early sixth century from the Corinthian colony of Corcyra, which used the same alphabet as its mother city—as, indeed, did most Corinthian colonies, either in a full or a modified form.[15] In addition, Corinthian vases carry numerous inscriptions explanatory of the figure scenes; these occur in the main on vases of the sixth-century black-figure period, and most museums contain some examples. But other vases carry dedicatory messages or other formulae, as for example *SEG* XIV 303, which occur also at earlier periods. The general type of the Corinthian alphabet was followed, with minor but distinctive differences, by the neighbouring cities of Sicyon and Megara.

A knowledge of the Attic alphabet is, of course, essential to a proper study of the official documents of the Periclean period and of the Peloponnesian War; but, although this is a major and indeed necessary period of study wherever the classics are cultivated, it is regrettable that absence of knowledge of how the Athenians expressed in letters the decrees they passed makes it necessary for such valuable documentary collections as M. N. Tod's *Greek Historical Inscriptions* to transcribe Attic texts into Ionic in order to make them intelligible. This is an obstacle to their appreciation as inscriptions, since, as will appear from subsequent chapters, many arguments based on them, especially where readings and restorations are concerned, cannot be understood except on the basis of the text as expressed in Attic lettering. In Fig. 3 the Ionic, Attic, and Corinthian alphabets are shown side by side. It should be noted that the forms shown are those, roughly speaking, of the early part of the fifth century. Where an earlier epichoric form had existed, it is shown in brackets before the listed letter; where subsequent development took place, it is shown in brackets after the letter concerned.

To complete this survey of the early alphabets and their development, it is necessary to introduce two additional points. Besides the development brought about by 'Ionic intrusion', there was also, as already stated, that which took place in the forms of the letters themselves, and this was further mentioned as a useful criterion on which a comparative chronology can be built up. The changes to newer forms did not take place everywhere at the same time. For example, in all regions the letter H, whether it represented the aspirate or long *e*, shows a development of form from ⊟ to H:

Ionic	Attic	Corinthian
(A) A	A	A
B	B	∫(B)
Γ	Λ	<C
Δ	Δ	Δ
(Ϝ)E	(Ϝ)E	B
-	-	F
I	I	I
(⊟)H(=η)	(⊟)H(='h')	(⊟)H('h')
(⊗)Θ	⊗(Θ)	⊗(Θ)
I	I	ϟ(I)
K	K	K
Λ	L	Λ
M	M	M
N	N	N
Ξ	XϹ	Ξ
O	O	O
Γ	Γ	Γ
-	-	M
(Q)	(Q)	Q
P	P	P
Σ	ϟ(Σ)	-
T	T	T
V(Y)	V(Y)	V(Y)
Φ	Φ	Φ
X	X	X
Ψ	ΦϹ	Ψ
Ω	-	-

Fig. 3. The epichoric alphabets of Ionia, Attica and Corinth *c.* 500 B.C. Earlier and later forms are shown in brackets respectively before and after the relevant letters.

Koppa did not outlast the sixth century in East Greece and Attica.

but the older form remained in some places for a longer time than in others, and because the new form appears in one city at a certain date that does not mean that all inscriptions from another city showing the older form must be assigned to a date earlier than that. In some cases the change-over is indeed roughly datable. In Corinth the crooked form of *iota* appears not to have outlasted the sixth century: in Athens the 'hot cross bun' type of *theta* does not long survive the Persian Wars, and the three-bar *sigma* was abandoned in the middle of the fifth century in favour of the variety with four strokes; while *upsilon* in the form V seems to have been especially popular in the period between 520 and 470 B.C. As a result, tables of epichoric alphabets show in many instances different forms for the same letter, in order to illustrate the changes that took place or to note coexistent varieties. It cannot be assumed that newer varieties immediately replaced the old, and some overlap of usage must always be allowed for. This overlap may be as much as a quarter of a century. The dedication of Peisistratus, son of Hippias, which Thucydides saw (VI, 54), is generally dated in 522/1 B.C., but the quality of its lettering is such that an early fifth-century date has been strongly advocated for it and, were the arguments confined to the epigraphy alone, this might have been found the more acceptable.[16]

Secondly, it is as well to notice the treatment of the 'spurious diphthongs', e.g. the contracted forms of ε + ε and ο + ο. These are familiar in the textbooks as ει and ου, but on Attic inscriptions they appear as simple E and O. Thus an Athenian document may use E to represent long *e*, short *e*, or the diphthong made of *e* plus *e*, and one must decide from the context which of the three is intended. The same is true of the use of O. This short version of the impure diphthongs lasted on beyond the adoption of the Ionic alphabet, and is to be found in existence well down the fourth century. By a false analogy the usage extended itself to places where it had no right to be. For example, the diphthong in τοῦτο is not in the category of those affected, and yet the spelling TOTO is not unusual in an Attic text. In Corinth, where the short and long *e* were alike represented by the strange *beta*-like form Ɓ, E was used to represent ει. The Attic usage was paralleled in Euboea, Ionia and elsewhere in the Aegean.

The fifth century saw the zenith and decline of the epichoric alphabets; by its end they were fast disappearing. But even though, as compared with the total amount of inscriptional material from Greece through the whole period of antiquity, the quantity of epichoric inscriptions is small, the period during which these local alphabets flourished was that of the most intense and productive development of Hellas, the period of which Herodotus and Thucydides are the chroniclers. The marked local differences they show, and the progressive attempts that were made to achieve some medium of expression common to all by the gradual and, in the end, universal acceptance of the Ionic alphabet, reflect in another way the stubborn parochialism of the Greeks and that essential unity, simultaneously felt, which made them aware that, despite local differences, they were bound together by a larger tie. Alphabetically the problem was resolved; politically the opposing tendencies continued to pull the Greeks in two directions, and the city-states were never able to accommodate their diversity and their unity in a workable system.

CHAPTER III

BOUSTROPHEDON AND STOICHEDON

IT has already been mentioned that the Phoenicians, from whom the Greeks derived their alphabet, wrote in the direction opposite to that natural to ourselves, that is, from right to left or (to us) backwards; this reverse direction is sometimes labelled as 'retrograde' or '*sinistrorsum*'. While some of the letters of the alphabet, such as *iota* or *tau*, are non-committal as regards direction, others such as B or E have a definitely 'forward-looking' character: but, when the Greeks first became acquainted with them, they or their equivalents at the time faced in the reverse direction, 𐊨 and 𐊝.[1] However, the Greeks soon discovered that the left-to-right direction for writing came easily to them and suited them as well as, if not better than, the direction they had originally learned, and in fact they were able to write in either direction with equal facility and intelligibility. Among the earliest Greek inscriptions known to us, some take the retrograde and others the normal left-to-right direction, entirely dependent, as it seems, on the choice of the writer. The graffito on the Dipylon jug, long among the most famous of early inscriptions, and the ominous warning to thieves on the little lekythos of Tataie from Cumae, are alike written from right to left, as is the more recently discovered graffito on a cup from Ischia promising not pains but pleasures to come.[2] The assorted sherds of early date discovered on Mount Hymettus show writing in both directions, but the majority of fragments, including those preserving the longest pieces of writing, have their messages written retrograde. The Mantiklos Apollo from Boeotia, which is to be dated soon after 700 B.C., has on its legs a dedication written in two horseshoe-shaped lines, the first from right to left and the second in the reverse direction.[3] A fragment of a plaque from Aegina to which, despite the developed appearance of the writing, it seems that a date even earlier than that of the Apollo must be assigned, shows the remains of a single line of inscription running from left to right.[4] All these are small-scale inscriptions scratched or painted on small objects of pottery or bronze. The earliest surviving stone-cut inscriptions seem to be the dedications to Hera discovered at Perachora near Corinth and known as the Perachora curbs. These dedications are written from right to left, as is the earliest inscription yet discovered in East Greece, the graffito of Dolion mentioned in the last chapter.[5]

That the direction of writing was, or swiftly became, immaterial is further illustrated by the figure scenes on vases. Here the names of the characters portrayed were, in archaic times, frequently written in near the figures concerned: on a heavily decorated vase the space was often somewhat limited, or available only in an awkward direction, and it seemed desirable also to put the initial letter of the name as close to the figure as was practicable. The names therefore run off in any direction in which there was room to write them, and there was a tendency to write the name of a leftward-facing figure in the same direction as the figure itself.

In fact, there seems to have been no difficulty in making writing fit the requirements of the moment, whatever they happened to be. The original choice of left-to-right or right-to-left was apparently the writer's own; after that, he could make his script curve around the contour of a vase, about the members of a statuette, or between the feet of a statue on the surface of a statue base.[6] It has been described as 'Snake-writing', *Schlangenschrift*,[7] and the name is not inappropriate. Nor was it necessary for the writing to be horizontal. Dedications were quite intelligible when written vertically up or down a statue or statuette, such as that dedicated by Mantiklos or the 'Kore'-type figure, also a dedication to Apollo, set up at the god's Delian sanctuary by Nicandra, which is one of the earliest examples of larger-scale Greek sculpture.[8] It was easy to complete such a dedication, should a second line of writing be required, simply by continuing the line of the script round at the end and back underneath the previous line. This was indeed more to the reader's convenience, especially if his ability to read were not marked; while picking his way from letter to letter and from word to word he did not have to interrupt the process at the end of the line, so that his eye could travel back to the point from which it had started. He could, on the contrary, keep going without a break, and, once one is used to the novelty, writing of this kind is actually quicker to read than writing of the conventional type.

The same method could, however, be used with equal effect on more regular surfaces designed solely for inscriptional use. So far we have been dealing with objects on which dedications were written, and on which, as a result, the writing had in some degree to be adapted to the surface available. But with slabs or blocks of stone set up or smoothed off for no other purpose than that writing should be put on them, the choice of method was freer. It was, for instance, more convenient both for inscriber and for reader that the inscription should be, as far as possible, in horizontal lines. It was not only easier to read and write, but it made a more economical use of the space. With the to-and-fro system of writing, the eye was never required to leave the stone for an instant, so that, with odd-numbered lines facing in one direction and even-numbered lines in the other, preserving the pattern for the whole of the inscription, it was possible to inscribe texts of considerable length with ease and complete intelligibility. Pausanias (v, 17, 6) says that writing of this kind was described as *boustrophedon* (βουστροφηδόν), since it turned at the end of each line as the ox turns with the plough at the end of each furrow. *Boustrophedon* has remained in use among epigraphists as a technical term for this style.

The accurate reproduction of a *boustrophedon* text in ordinary epigraphic type on the printed page of a modern book presents something of a difficulty, since it is hardly feasible for the printer or intelligible for the reader to print alternate lines of Greek backwards. The most usual device used by editors is to warn the reader, by a note in the introductory remarks or at the side of the text itself, that what follows is written *boustrophedon*, and then to print every line in the ordinary way, from left to right. Against the first two lines it is customary to set arrows (→, ←) indicating the actual direction which the writing as inscribed on the stone takes, it being understood that subsequent lines preserve the same direction, and that lines 3, 5, 7, etc., will face the same way as line 1, while lines 4, 6, 8, etc., will be of the same kind as line 2. As a ready example the *boustrophedon* fragments *SEG* XII 2–3 will serve as well as any.

In the course of time it seems to have been acknowledged that the left-to-right direction was the more natural and intelligible, and the necessity of breaking off the process of reading at the end of each line was apparently felt as a minor disadvantage compared with that of having to learn to read in two directions. Most people are right-handed, and for them it is easier to pull strokes from left to right, in the process of writing, than it is to push them from right to left. The old style, also, was incompatible with a new feeling for the artistic layout of an inscription, which took shape in the *stoichedon* style of writing, about which more will be said below. At all events, whatever the reason for the change, the *boustrophedon* style was by degrees abandoned during the sixth century. Since, however, many inscriptions dealt with religious matters, either as recording dedications or as regulating the cult practices, while others recorded the laws of the state, or the local *fasti*, all of which had at least a quasi-religious significance, they had acquired a certain sanctity in their *boustrophedon* form, and the result is that some sacral inscriptions and calendars are still written in that form even in the fifth century; the style also lingered on the longest in the epigraphically most conservative part of Greece, Crete. A calendar from Miletus, one of the most progressive cities of the time, which is of a date little earlier than the very end of the sixth century, is still in the *boustrophedon* style; a column from Thera, apparently containing some record of cult regulations, belongs to the first part of the fifth century, as do the fragments from the Athenian Agora, already cited, which have a similar content.[9] Thereafter the style does not reappear. But in Crete it was still favoured in the middle of the fifth century, and it has left its most impressive monument there in the great law code of Gortyn. This code makes use of regular and up-to-date forms for the individual letters, polished and artistic versions of the old Gortynian epichoric, which compare favourably with the letter-forms and general epigraphic quality of the inscribed documents which the young Athenian democracy was just beginning to record in such numbers. But the whole code, from first to last, is written in the *boustrophedon* style, with alternate lines facing in opposite directions.[10] It may be that this was a conscious archaism, for it is noteworthy that the subject of the inscription is a code of law, and it may have been thought desirable to retain the old style as more august and traditional. But the quantity of *boustrophedon* fragments of earlier date from the same site seems to suggest that the great code stood at the end of a long series of inscriptions in the old style, which had remained unaffected by the more modern fashions prevalent elsewhere in the Greek world. The retention of the epichoric script argues in the same direction. But this insulation did not last much longer, and Crete too adopted both the consistent left-to-right direction of writing and the Ionic script.

Although writing from left to right had, by the fifth century, become almost everywhere the rule, differentiation between successive lines of an inscription evidently had some aesthetic attraction. At least, this seems the only reasonable explanation of the occasional practice, attested now by more than one example from the Hellenistic period, of the use of two colours in colouring the inscribed letters of a text.[11] It is well known that, for greater clarity, stone-cut letters were often also coloured with paint, as is in fact not infrequent in modern times. The colours have for obvious reasons seldom survived, but where traces do remain they suggest that red was the colour ordinarily used for the purpose. Where two colours were used, alternate lines were painted in red and black. This two-colour system may have been more widespread than the scanty remains of it so far found suggest, and the chances of the survival of paint traces on an inscription are too low for hopes that more evidence will be speedily forthcoming.

It is perhaps worth noting, at this point, that inscriptions, in whatever direction they were written, were generally written continuously, that is to say, without any break between words or between clauses or sentences. The major exceptions to this general rule are dedications or grave inscriptions in which the text is short and where it has been thought artistically preferable to arrange the words in some symmetrical pattern—the practice generally followed in printed notices or inscriptions of the present time. This did demand some spatial arrangement, and often called, for instance, for the emphasis or isolation in a separate line of the name of the god to whom the dedication was made. On a grave stele the relevant information was frequently inscribed with a single line given to each word; if the stele commemorated two persons, the inscriptions might be set in two parallel columns with a blank space between them to differentiate them. But in ordinary public documents the writing ran on without a break, line after line. The division of it into words, when these documents are transcribed for our own purposes into the Greek type of the textbooks, is a matter of convenience for ourselves, and to that extent the printed texts fail to reproduce the true character of the inscription as it exists on the stone.

Some use was, however, made of punctuation, especially in the archaic period. At that time it consisted of a pattern of dots, either two, as in a colon, or three set one above the other. To mark a particular division even six, set in two columns of three, might be used.[12] These divided groups of words, rather than individual words from their neighbours. But the practice died out, and was not again revived until the Roman period, when, following the Roman custom of marking divisions between words, some decorative sign was on occasions introduced for the same purpose in inscriptions written in Greek. This might be no more than a small triangular mark, but frequently, and especially in the Hadrianic period, might be more elaborately expressed with an ivy leaf or some similar device.

It has sometimes been thought that the early history of Greek epigraphy can be divided roughly into three periods, the first when the direction of writing was exclusively from right to left, on the Phoenician model, the second covering a transitional *boustrophedon* style which, while tending towards the more natural left-to-right direction, was not yet prepared to abandon the old way entirely, and finally a third period, in which the left-to-right direction was universally followed. This 'third period' is not in dispute, since that was, in fact, the final and permanent development of Greek writing, but it is doubtful whether the variable practices of the early centuries of Greek epigraphic history can be moulded into so convenient a pattern. As far as single-line inscriptions go, it is never possible to say, even at the earliest period, that they were exclusively written from right to left, and among the earliest examples of Greek inscriptions are instances in which the writer adopted the normal and, later, canonical left-to-right direction. Examples of inscriptions of more than one line earlier than 600 B.C. are too few for any chronological pattern to be suggested. A kind of *boustrophedon* appears very early on the Mantiklos Apollo, and the question seems simply to have been one of continuing with the writing in the nearest and most convenient space. Inscriptions such as those on Tataie's lekythos or the Ischia cup, while being written in more than one line round the vases, nevertheless consist of a continuous line of writing which goes in a spiral. There is thus no hard and fast differentiation between a 'first period' and a 'second period'. Early practices of writing were fluid and variable, and it was not until the Greeks began to set up inscriptions intended purely and simply as such, rather than those which were merely descriptive adjuncts to dedications and the like, that epigraphic method began to crystallise—first into the monumental *boustrophedon* style and then into the consistent left-to-right direction.

It must also be borne in mind that speed of literary development differed in different places. This has already been particularly emphasised in the case of Crete, but it occurred in varying degrees elsewhere. It is thus dangerous to argue from the development of inscriptional practice in Attica, the best known area, to that of less progressive regions. Much would also depend on the predilections of the engraver and of his client, on the character of the inscription, and also on the stone-cutter's age. An older man would perhaps be likely to cling to the forms and methods of an earlier period which a younger stone-cutter, working at the same time, would have abandoned in favour of the more modern fashions. The seventh and sixth centuries are, therefore, centuries of continuing transition, during which all parts of Greece went through a longer or shorter *boustrophedon* period as far as inscriptions of any length were concerned: but any chronological suggestions should be based only on a comparative study of the material from the area in question, in which numerous other criteria, besides that of the direction of the writing, must play a full part.

If '*boustrophedon*' is one technical term which requires explanation for the student of epigraphy, there is a second, very similar to it, which also needs some discussion, namely, '*stoichedon*'. The *stoichedon* style was the subject of a monograph written just before the Second World War by R. P. Austin,[13] and to this it is advisable to turn for a more complete account of it. What follows can do no more than outline the main conclusions about it to which Austin came on the basis of his comprehensive survey. As to what 'the *stoichedon* style' means, it is worth quoting Austin's introductory paragraph, where the matter is put quite succinctly:

'The stoichedon style of engraving in Greek inscriptions is that style in which the letters are in alinement vertically as well as horizontally, and are placed at equal intervals along their respective alinements. It has been aptly compared to a military formation, where the number and position of the men in the front rank determine the number and position of the men in each rank behind. Thus in a perfect *stoichedon* inscription the number of letters in each line is the same, and every new line falls letter by letter underneath the line above.'

The letters are written in fact κατὰ στοίχους, in rows, and it has already been mentioned that the development of such a pattern requires that all letters face the same way. Its incompatibility with the *boustrophedon* style of writing is clearly seen in Attic material of the middle of the sixth century,[14] in which a growing tendency to set vertical strokes, such as *iota*, directly underneath one another is defeated when letters such as *epsilon* face in different directions from their initial vertical. The adoption of a consistent left-to-right direction of writing brought the *stoichedon* style to a rapid maturity by the end of the century, and it was the style in which the inscriptions of the classical period were with few exceptions cut.

While Austin's discussion makes it unnecessary to give a substantial account of the style here, and those who wish to examine it more closely are well advised to turn to his detailed study, it is as well to go briefly into one or two salient points. Firstly, the *geographical extent* of the style. It is best known to us from Athens, which provides by far the greatest number of examples. It was in fact, as was mentioned a moment ago, the principal inscriptional style in Attica from the end of the sixth century to the end of the fourth. But it was by no means confined to Attica, although in the remainder of Greece its use varied. In the Peloponnese, for example, it was infrequently used, and the majority of the Peloponnesian examples come from a single source, Epidaurus, which is near enough to Athens to have been susceptible to Athenian epigraphic influence. From the rest of the Peloponnese barely two dozen examples are cited. North of Attica, a number of examples occur among inscriptions from the sanctuary of Amphiaraus at Oropus, but Oropus, although reckoned as within the boundaries of Boeotia, was controlled by Athens for much of the period during which the *stoiche-*

don style flourished; apart from Oropus, Boeotia in general has little to offer. The largest number of non-Attic *stoichedon* texts from the Greek mainland come from Delphi, to which may be added a sprinkling from the rest of the surrounding district of Phocis, principally from Elatea. Elsewhere in European Greece instances appear to be few and scattered. Among the islands, Delos used the style regularly while under Athenian control, as might have been expected, while in Melos the series of grave inscriptions, some of which are illustrated in Fig. 2, also makes use of the same style. Otherwise, examples both in the Aegean and on the coast of Asia Minor are relatively few. It emerges that the style, while not exclusively Attic, was for the most part under Attic influence, Delphi being the only independent user of it. But the Delphic sanctuary, like the Athenian democracy, had a large inscriptional output, and the style was a good one for rapid production.

Secondly, the *duration of the style*. Although mainly Attic in its use, the origin of *stoichedon* writing may well be considered as non-Attic. At any rate, a dedication made by two Perinthians in Samos in about 580–570 B.C. (*SEG* XII 391), while not fully *stoichedon*, is certainly inclining to the style, and the well-known dedication of Aeakes, also from Samos, is as early as all, or nearly all, the earliest Attic *stoichedon* texts.[15] Megara also provides examples of the early fifth century, when Attic *stoichedon* was just getting into its stride. Apart from that, the style outside Attica is most frequently met with in the fourth and early third centuries, towards the close of its period of dominance in Attica itself.

Within Attica the style came into being in the latter part of the sixth century, and continued thereafter until the beginning of the third. After that it declined very rapidly, and by the end of the third quarter of the same century had to all intents and purposes ceased to exist. A few isolated texts inscribed in the *stoichedon* style may be cited from both inside and outside Attica later than that period. The latest and perhaps most notable of these is the long inscription from Oenoanda in Lycia, of the beginning of the third century A.D., which records the genealogy of Licinnia Flavilla and Diogenes of that city;[16] but exceptions are always something of a surprise, and do not invalidate the overall hypothesis that for the *stoichedon* style in general 225 B.C. or thereabouts should be considered as a *terminus ante quem*.

To transcribe *stoichedon* texts for ordinary working purposes it is best to use paper already divided into squares and to set a letter of the text into each successive square, thus reproducing the pattern of the inscription itself. This in fact resembles the engraver's own method of work. The stoneworker drew on the stone, on which the inscription was to be cut, a regular pattern of horizontal and vertical lines at equi-distant intervals. He might do this in chalk or in some other medium which he could easily obliterate afterwards. Sometimes he might incise the lines lightly on the stone, and traces of guide-lines may sometimes be seen in the background of surviving inscriptions, both those en-graved *stoichedon* and those which needed only horizontal and not vertical guides.[17] Having drawn out his grid, he would then set the letters of his text consecutively in the squares, rather as the letters appear in a modern crossword puzzle, or else he would use the inter-sections of the lines as the centre points of his letters, which would produce the same pattern and the same intervals. Horizontally the centre of each letter was equidistant from those of its immediate neighbours, and vertically the spaces between the letters remained con-stant, with the letters in one line appearing exactly below those in the line above it and above those in the line below. The same effect is pro-duced by the typewriter, which writes everything in a consistent *stoichedon* pattern, although word-division prevents the same regularity at the end of the line as in a Greek *stoichedon* inscription. Since the texts were, for the most part, inscribed continuously, without punctuation and without spaces between the words, the whole inscribed area was completely filled with a regular and uniform pattern of letters. The same number of letters stood in each line, and this, it may easily be seen, is a valuable aid in the restoration of mutilated inscriptions, a matter which will be discussed in a subsequent chapter. Once the length of one line of a *stoichedon* inscription can be established, the length of every line is known, and a knowledge of the number of letters missing in a broken text will govern any restoration which may attempt to remedy the deficiency.

Inscriptions are sometimes referred to as being 'quasi-*stoichedon*'. This merely indicates that the *stoichedon* pattern is not rigidly applied throughout. It may be a case, such as that early example from Samos already mentioned, in which there is a tendency to *stoichedon* which is not followed through. It may imply that, while the general style of the inscription is that of the regular *stoichedon* (i.e., it has a *stoichedon* 'feeling'), nevertheless the stoneworker did not plot it out on the basis of a regular grid pattern and, with only his artistic sensibility to guide him, has failed to keep rigidly to the uniformity of writing which is characteristic of the style at its best. Or it may be, simply, that for one reason or another, perhaps to put emphasis on a particular word or line, or perhaps through difficulties of space, the number of letters in one or two lines varies slightly from the number in the rest. Even so, the number of letters per line in a quasi-*stoichedon* inscription must be regarded as constant within very narrow limits.

It is however necessary to bear in mind two factors which sometimes upset the regularity of what is intended to be a rigid *stoichedon* text, and which put a check on the assurance with which restorations of missing parts of a *stoichedon* inscription may be proposed. In the later ·fifth century the Attic engravers began to find objections to a system which compelled them to divide words like τε or δέ between one line and the next, or to divide a longer word or a name absurdly, as for instance Περικλέ|ς. They preferred to break a word at the completion of a syllable, even if that meant leaving one or two letter spaces untenanted at the end of a line. For example, they might decide to write τὸ ν|δὲ φσέφισμα rather than the τὸ δ|ὲ φσέφισμα which an absolutely rigid *stoichedon* pattern requires, or, instead of Περικλέ|ς, they would prefer to break the name half way and write Περι*νν*|κλ̄ς. This interruption of the strict pattern of a *stoichedon* text in order to break the words at the ends of the lines more naturally is known as the principle of 'syllabic division'. Syllabic division is found very little on the ordinary decrees of the βουλή and δῆμος, but is not infrequent in inventories, records of disbursements of funds, and other accounting documents, in which it continued in use in the fourth century. But since it is occasionally met with in other types of record also, it cannot be safely ignored as a possible intervening factor when a *stoichedon* inscription is being studied. Occurrences of it, as will be seen from the examples above, are noted in the printed text with *vacat* signs, each *v* indicating a single uninscribed letter space.

Austin believed that the incompatibility of syllabic division and the strict requirements of the rigid *stoichedon* style did much to contribute to the decline of the style as a whole. Syllabic division becomes common in all types of inscription once the style is abandoned. Against this view it may be noted that, when the style was at its best and most popular, syllabic division was for the most part confined to one class of document, and that in any case, in a text in which the lines are long and in which the letters are fairly small, as was frequently the case in the fourth century, the absence of one or two letters at the end of the line can go relatively unnoticed. More important in the style's decline were artistic considerations in the general layout of the text. Aesthetically each one must judge the *stoichedon* style for himself. At its best, as shown on Plate 2, it is remarkably attractive in the artistic sense; but it can become tiresome if it remains completely uncompromising. One of its cardinal weaknesses, from this point of view, is the disproportionate amount of space it gives to the letter *iota*, which is set in a square by itself no less than a 'wide' letter such as M, and which, as a result, leaves an awkwardly wide extent of blank stone between itself and the letters on either side of it. *Tau*, wide at the top but narrow below, also fits unhappily into the *stoichedon* pattern. The result is that the regular pattern gives an impression of irregularity, and the total effect is often unsatisfactory. Equally awkward for the style was the increasing use of tapering rather than rectangular stelae for inscriptions. The rigid *stoichedon* pattern demands a rectangular field, but stelae which had a slight taper towards the top were artistically a pleasing variant on the plain rectangle. It is instructive, in this connexion, to compare Plate 1 with Plate 3. But the tapered stele produced complications for the *stoichedon* style, which could be adapted to it only with difficulty, by the introduction of new vertical columns at each side of the text as the inscription progressed and the stele became wider. The use of tapered stelae grew in popularity towards the end of the fourth century, significantly just before the rapid decline of the *stoichedon* style set in. But *IG* I^2 22, of the middle of the fifth century, illustrated in Plate 1, provides an early example of the difficulties encountered in accommodating the *stoichedon* pattern to a stone which was not rectangular, and this was not a happy augury for the future.[18] It is therefore necessary to make sure, as far as possible, of the general shape of the stone on which a *stoichedon* text is inscribed. If it proves that the right and left edges are not parallel, and that the stele therefore tapered, one must be prepared for some difficulties and interruptions in the strict succession of the *stoichoi*.

Since the period of dominance of this style coincided with the classical period of the Greek city-state, the period which is the principal subject of study for most Hellenists, it is as well to be fully conversant with it. It is perhaps possible to see, in the love of order which it shows, and also in the inflexibility which it imposes on those who adopt it, something of the general atmosphere of the world in which it flourished. The artistic qualities of a plain inscription, as will be shown in a later chapter, may reflect, in a small way, the *ethos* of their period no less than the larger works of art more generally regarded as such. At least it is not too much to suggest that, through their appearance as well as through their content, the spirit and will of the Athenian democracy of the fifth and fourth centuries continue to live and breathe through the inscribed records that it has left behind.

CHAPTER IV

THE CLASSIFICATION OF INSCRIPTIONS

SINCE Greek epigraphic texts provide evidence of some kind or another for practically every aspect of Greek life and society, the same text is frequently a useful citation, on several counts, for a number of points of interest. This being so, any attempt to catalogue them or differentiate them by types, or according to their content, must in many cases prove arbitrary or unsatisfactory. But some order has to be introduced into the wealth of inscriptional material if it is to be used with any ease, so that some system of categories is necessary, within which the sorted epigraphic evidence becomes much more manageable. Broadly speaking this can be done without too much difficulty: public decrees are easily distinguishable from tomb-epitaphs, and the majority of inscriptions can be assigned without trouble to basic categories of this kind, even though, when all is done, a residue of '*varia*' or '*fragmenta incerta*' never fails to be left over. Some inscriptions are so fragmentary or mutilated or otherwise uninformative that no definite assignment is possible. Most of the collections of epigraphic texts therefore subdivide the inscriptions into broadly based categories, within which they are generally arranged in the chronological order of the dates to which they belong or may be thought to belong.[1] An exception to this general rule concerns grave inscriptions, which may be catalogued alphabetically according to the first letter of the name of the deceased, without reference to the date to which the monument is to be ascribed.[2] Collections of texts which themselves select inscriptions, perhaps of a single type, for a particular purpose, to illustrate some aspect of history or society, may list their material in chronological order irrespective of category, or they may adopt some other policy to suit the special programme which they are following. But where this selective element is lacking, and where it is simply a matter of putting in order all the inscriptions belonging to one particular area or found in one particular excavation, it is necessary to be prepared to recognise the category to which a text belongs, so that it may be readily identified and placed with kindred material, where those who want to make use of it will know where to find it and will know what to expect.

One conventional and very broad division sometimes used is that between 'public' and 'private' inscriptions, although these terms are perhaps a little old-fashioned nowadays. 'Public' inscriptions, as one might guess, comprise all the official transactions of the state, or similar transactions of the subdivisions of the state such as demes or tribes—decrees, treaties, financial accounts, records of treasure, building specifications, public dedications to the gods or statues erected or other honours paid by the public authority to some deserving citizen or foreigner, public memorials for those fallen in battle, and so forth. In fact, every aspect of the state's activities may somehow and somewhere be recorded on stone, and the field which this general category may cover is extremely wide. Among 'private' inscriptions the largest single group is undoubtedly that formed by tombstones and funerary monuments, but the category also includes private dedications, private legal documents such as wills or manumissions of slaves, as well as property contracts such as transfers or mortgages, statues or other monuments erected for private purposes at the expense of an individual, and finally a great many 'personal' inscriptions such as marks of ownership, incantations and curses (*tabellae defixionum*), and a variety of similar items. The subdivisions could be multiplied, but within these broad limits it is possible to make a preliminary sorting of the material, and most inscriptions fall naturally into the one grouping or the other.

Within the 'public' and 'private' grouping they may then be allotted more narrowly to the types of inscription, some of which have been cited above, to which they appear to belong on the basis of their detailed content. It is worth noting that particular types may occur more frequently in one place than in another, and a knowledge of the provenience of a text may, in cases of doubt, prove helpful in suggesting what kind of an inscription it might be. For example, the sanctuary of Asclepius at Epidaurus has produced, as would be expected, a large number of dedications to the god and divinities associated with him; there is also a series of texts recording medical cures performed by the god, as well as some important records of expenditure relating to the building of the great temple in the fourth century.[3] But this was not the place for burials, and discoveries of funerary inscriptions in the neighbourhood have therefore been few. Similarly, the sanctuary at Delphi has produced great numbers of dedications, but here the decrees of the Delphic Amphictyony and of the Delphians themselves are also numerous, since the place had a political entity and an international importance beyond that merely of a place of worship. The Athenian Agora has proved a most notable site for the discovery of legislation of the Athenian democracy, it being the centre of urban life and a place where it was natural to set up the records for the perusal of the citizens. In the Kerameikos, on the other hand, outside the Dipylon gate, the character of the discoveries is entirely different, for there was a considerable cemetery here, and the inscriptions found in that area almost entirely relate, in consequence, to funerary monuments. In assigning a doubtful case to its proper category, it is therefore necessary to bear in mind the context in which it was found and the type of inscription that one might expect the context to produce.

In the majority of instances the type of the inscription is readily recognisable, since the general characteristics of each type are usually reproduced throughout Greece, with variations in detail but with an overall similarity. The major collections of inscriptions, and notably the *Corpus* (for which see Chapter IX below), classify the material under standard headings, *Decreta, Catalogi, Tituli honorarii, Tituli sepulcrales*, and the like, so that all inscriptions of a given type from a given site may be found together; the same order of categories is maintained for each site, so that it is not difficult to set one's hand on the material of the same character found elsewhere. It may be useful to glance briefly at some of the types of inscription which may most commonly be met with, at any rate by those who use epigraphy as ancillary to historical or other studies, and to notice what features are particularly characteristic about them. There is no need to elaborate the more obvious points— for example, that dedications may be recognised because some verb of dedication may appear as the operative word in them, or that a manumission will somewhere contain some such phrase as 'I set free' or 'I dedicate to the god with the intention of freeing'. But there are other points of detail which are less obvious, and while it is possible to discuss only a few of them, those few may be regarded as basic material on which the reader may elaborate for himself from larger epigraphic studies and from his own progressive experience.[4]

Decrees. Greek states varied in the amount of their public decisions that they committed to the permanent record of a stone-cut inscription. The amount of such material discovered at Athens should not lead us to assume either that a similar bulk was reproduced elsewhere, even in other democracies, or that *all* Athenian public business was so inscribed. Much was left by the Athenians in the more perishable papyrus of the archives in the Metroon, or on whitened boards (λευκώματα) intended only for a temporary record. In other cities political interest or financial possibility governed the publication of the affairs of state, but the example set by the Athenians did produce a steady growth of permanent record in other parts of Greece in the fourth and third centuries, and the practice was taken over by cities and states in the west and north, as they gradually developed their political entities, as well as in the Hellenised areas of the east opened up by Alexander's conquests.

Decrees of the βουλή and δῆμος at Athens, or their equivalents elsewhere, usually begin with some introductory formula, varying in detail from place to place and from period to period, but with common and unmistakable characteristics. This may simply say that this is a decision of the people, or the council, or the assembly, or whatever the appropriate body may be, and a straightforward type is shown as example 1 below. The classic example of the formula is that most familiar from the decrees of the Athenians as the introduction of the assembly's decision: Ἔδοξε τῇ βουλῇ καὶ τῷ δήμῳ. In the fourth and later centuries a variant formula with δεδόχθαι may be used, but the basis remains the same. Similar phraseology will be met with elsewhere, varying according to the local constitution and according to local practice. This formula is frequently, in Attica regularly, immediately followed by a mention of the date, of the magistrate or magistrates presiding, and of the proposer of the decree. It is on the verb of proposing or saying involved in this last item (ὁ δεῖνα εἶπε) that the text of the main body of the decree grammatically depends, and this follows on in a continuous accusative and infinitive construction of *oratio obliqua*. The operative verb of the decree, what the people have in fact decided to do, is therefore in the infinitive, but between it and the mention of the proposer which introduces it there may intervene a long subordinate clause, giving the reasons for the proposal having been put forward and for the people's decision—as in *IG* I² 118, illustrated on Pl. 2, in which Διειτρέφης εἶπε in line 6 is really followed, as the operative word, by ἐπαινέσαι in line 12, the purport of the decree of Diitrephes being to thank Oeniades and to write him down as a public benefactor. But between the two comes a long clause introduced by ἐπειδή explaining why Oeniades has been thought worthy of this distinguished treatment. The inscriptions shown in Plates 1 and 3 are unusual in that the one records the decision of a body of commissioners for the affairs of Miletus and the other is a law recommended by a special body of lawgivers (νομοθέται). But the preambles are in both cases similar to that discussed as a standard type.

It is the almost invariable practice, when not ἔδοξε but δεδόχθαι or ἐψηφίσθαι is used, for the subordinate explanatory clause to *precede* the verb of decision (ἐπειδή..., δεδόχθαι). At other times, although not earlier than the fourth century, the preamble of the decree may be reinforced, as is the case in the decree on Pl. 3, by some expression of good wishes or good fortune for the body taking the decision—a wish, presumably, that all may come out well in the matter on which the decree has been passed—ἀγαθῇ τύχῃ τῷ δήμῳ τῷ Ἀθηναίων.

Finally, the decree in honour of Oeniades shows, well spaced out at the top and preceding everything else, the single word θεοί. This occurs frequently in this position and, as it seems, rather cryptically indicates that, before the matter under discussion was considered and decided upon, the proper religious exercises had been performed or invocations made.

The same decree gives a good illustration, in the body of the text which follows, of a regular type of decree, generally known as an 'honorary decree', giving thanks and honours of one kind or another to a citizen or alien who has deserved well of the state. In later centuries they tended to become more elaborate and fulsome than this, and the gratitude was often displayed in greater material rewards, but again the basic type remains constant and the expressions follow the same kind of formula as is shown here. In lines 26 and following may also be seen the standard method of expressing the moving and adoption of an amendment. The decree to be voted upon came before the assembly as a *probouleuma*, in a draft presented and approved by the βουλή. When it received the people's approval it became a ψήφισμα. But it was open for any citizen to propose its amendment, and he did so by expressing agreement with the βουλή, or with any previous amenders, as far as the general matter went, but in some specific detail he proposed something different. On the stone this involves another verb of saying, by way of introduction, and then a μέν . . . δέ construction, τὰ μὲν ἄλλα καθάπερ τῇ βουλῇ, and δέ introducing the operative infinitive which will describe the amended action to be taken. In this case Antichares moved, as an amendment, that Oeniades should be described in the resolution (which in its other terms he accepted) not as of Sciathus but as of Old Sciathus, and, as line 7 shows, his amendment was acted upon when the *psephisma* in its final form was entered in the records.[5]

The development of the preamble through the period of classical antiquity is discussed in Chapter v below, and examples 2 and 3 at the end of this chapter will illustrate the elements already described. It is from this basis that the decree, whatever the nature of its contents or the subject with which it is concerned, will proceed, and this fundamental uniformity is of the greatest value in allocating to its type even a small fragment which appears to fit with it. With experience the phraseology both of preamble and of the contents of decrees (such as honorary decrees) of a recurrent type becomes reasonably clear to recognise.

Inventories, catalogues, building accounts, expenditure accounts.
The general character of all these is that of a simple list with a heading to
indicate what the list is about and, where disbursements of money are
concerned, a note of the amount plus a record of the reason why it was
made and the person or persons to whom it was made. In the inventories of the temple treasures, which are in fact an authoritative check of
the items handed over by one board of treasurers to its successors in
office, there is some introductory formula of a type such as 'This is what
the treasurers (of, e.g., Athena), in the year of *w*, when *x* was secretary,
handed on to the board of treasurers consisting of *y* and his colleagues'.
Expenditure accounts, when the disbursements were made from a
reserve fund such as that, in the later fifth century, kept on the Athenian
acropolis, have a similar heading: 'This is what the treasurers (of
Athena) disbursed, the board, that is, consisting of *ζ* and his colleagues.'
The tribute lists of the period of the first Athenian empire, recording
the sixtieth of the *phoros* paid over to the treasury of Athena, have
headings recording the *Hellenotamiai* in office and responsible for the
transaction. Building records, although so called, are in fact similar
records of expenditure for the treasurer-year, listing item by item each
expense as it occurred, from one prytany to the next, and the result is to
provide an illuminating account, recording each detail as it came up, of
the actual process of construction of some of the great monuments of
ancient architecture, some of them still surviving. The best example of
this kind for further study is the record of expenditure on the Erechtheum at Athens, which is a mine of architectural and social history as
well as an imposing monument for the epigraphist.[6]

'Catalogues' may be of a strict inventory type, like the naval catalogues from mid-fourth century Athens, which consisted of a complete check of the ships and naval equipment, the persons responsible
for them, and a note of their serviceable or unserviceable condition.
Other catalogues may list people or members of official boards or
groups, and some of them more or less amount to honorary decrees.
For example, it became a frequent practice in Athens and elsewhere to
pass a vote of commendation in recognition of outstanding merit shown
by magistrates during their period of office, or by the youths undergoing
military training (*epheboi*). Such decrees were liable to include a complete nominal roll of the officials or ephebes so commended, including,
in the latter case, the officers responsible for their training and conduct.
Some of these decrees are very long and detailed (see, for example,
SEG xv 104). On the other hand, the preamble to the list of names
may be relatively short, or the list may have been drawn up for some

other purpose, or the only part of the whole inscription which survives may come from the list, without any further clue regarding the character of the complete text. As a result, it is not always clear whether records of this kind belong to the category of *Decreta* or of *Catalogi*, since they contain the characteristics of both. Athenian examples of the ephebic lists, for instance, are divided among both groupings. The practice of inscribing such lists continued over a long period at Athens, and here again the changes and developments which took place in the method of expressing them are often guides to their date.

Dedications. If they contain the word ἀνέθηκε or its equivalent, these, as remarked above, are easily identified. The same is true if, even in default of this operative word, some other dedicatory term, such as χαριστήριον, is introduced. But there are many permutations and combinations of phraseology which occur in this type of inscription, and one cannot count on finding such direct clues as this. The verb, for example, may be totally omitted, although its presence is implied, in an inscription which shows the dedicator's name in the nominative case, the object dedicated in the accusative, and, in the dative, the recipient of the honour. Of these three components the second may be omitted, and indeed the first also, leaving the inscription composed entirely of the recipient in the dative; but the dedicants usually included a reference to themselves, as a form of justifiable self-advertisement. Another form, serving the same purpose, sets the name of the recipient in the genitive case, indicating simply that the object dedicated is now the god's property (e.g., 'of Zeus'). And, especially in the early period, the object dedicated may speak for itself, and say 'I am (the property) of (e.g. Zeus)'. Sometimes, though rarely (e.g. *SEG* XI 905), the name of the deity stands alone, as a simple announcement, in the nominative case.

Finally, some reason for making the dedication may be added by the grateful devotee. He may have been instructed by the god himself, in a dream or an oracle, to make it, and in that case will add some such phrase as κατὰ μαντείαν or κατὰ πρόσταγμα; or he may add details of some disease or danger from which the god has saved him. But the reason may be no more than a desire to accord to the god the praise that is his due, for which the accusative εὐχήν is often a sufficient indication.

Dedications occur both in verse and in prose; verse dedications were especially favoured in the archaic period, when they were at their simplest, neatest, and most expressive, with a wealth of variations on the standard themes. Those from the Athenian Acropolis which belong to the period down to the Persian Wars have been edited and discussed in a single volume by A. E. Raubitschek.[7] A complete collection of dedications in verse is planned for a forthcoming volume of W. Peek's *Griechische Vers-Inschriften*. It is worth noting that the arrangement of dedicatory inscriptions frequently departs from the usual type of the continuous text, and uses spacing and symmetrical design in order to emphasise the name of dedicant or recipient, or any other feature which is regarded as of importance. The appearance of symmetrical arrangement on an otherwise unplaceable fragment may at least suggest that it belongs with this category, and it is essential to pay due regard to the symmetry in proposing any restoration for the missing parts of such a piece.

Tituli honorarii. Some dispute may arise in this section, as in that concerned with lists and catalogues, as to when an inscription is properly to be included under this heading and when it is not. Honorary decrees, such as that for Oeniades of Sciathus, can be regarded from some points of view as belonging to this class, and yet they are regularly classified not here but under *Decreta*. Similarly some inscriptions, intended as a mark of honour, have also the character of a dedication and contain the word ἀνέθηκε. Indeed, the statue, or whatever it may be, can be doing a double service as an honour to the person portrayed and a dedication to the gods. But this is a convenient category for the numerous statue bases, inscriptions on buildings or other objects, and a variety of texts which sought to do honour to local or foreign benefactors, even though it may be difficult at times to decide whether they might not be better included among decrees or dedications. To put up a statue to someone who had done good to the city (or who, it was hoped, *would* do so if treated in the right way) was a regular feature of Greek political life in the Hellenistic and Roman periods. It does not occur in the fifth century, and hardly in the fourth, but from then on the well-being of a Greek city depended on people and circumstances outside its own confines, and generosity in the bestowing of honours was a tactic of politics that had its uses. *Tituli honorarii* may however have a private, as well as a public, origin; statues were sometimes erected by individuals, to commemorate members of their own family who they thought deserved commemoration, or to acknowledge benefactors in a handsome way, or to pay judicious honour to the reigning emperor or local dynast.

In such inscriptions the person represented is generally set in the accusative case, with the public body or private individual bestowing the honours or showing the gratitude appearing in the nominative. The verb (ἀνέστησε or the like) may be expressed but is more commonly omitted. If the inscription also serves as a dedication, the god concerned will appear in the dative. In the case of buildings, which were in the Roman period frequently inscribed with an expression of honour towards the emperor of the time, the inscription is again something of a dedication, and the emperor's name appears in the dative case, sometimes with no further expression either of the people bestowing the honour or of the thing which was intended as the mark of honour, both presumably being self-evident. But the first or both of these may be added. This usage is very much the same as that appearing in Latin inscriptions, and may have been to some extent affected by it.

This type of inscription may include some expression of the reason for erecting the statue, generally expressed in vague terms such as 'on account of personal excellence and good-will' or something similar. Occasionally something more fulsome may be expressed, and it is also worth mentioning that, where public works are concerned, the magistrate or other person responsible for them may also be recorded.

Under this heading it may be as well to refer to the inscriptions which occur in connexion with the statues of victors in the games, especially those associated with the great sanctuaries such as Olympia, where the record of his athletic prowess was often inscribed on the base of the statue of the victor concerned. But these records are perhaps better to be grouped with others referring to contests both athletic and dramatic, under the general heading of *Tituli agonistici*.

On statue bases in the category just described, as well as on those more properly classed as dedications, it is not infrequent that the artist of the work may have added his name. These artists' signatures represent some of our firmest and most direct evidence for the work of sculptors, some of them already well known to the history of art from literary sources but many of them mere names otherwise unattested, who were commissioned to produce the wealth of statuary with which the cities and sanctuaries bristled. Where such signatures occur on fragments which cannot otherwise be assigned, they are sometimes grouped in a separate category of *Signaturae artificum*, along with signatures of potter or painter on vases. But if the total inscription reveals itself as a dedication or something similar, that category generally takes the precedence: artists' signatures may therefore have to be looked for under a variety of categories. However, J. Marcadé's *Recueil des signatures de sculpteurs grecs* aims to provide a complete and separate record of them which will overcome this difficulty.

Tituli sepulcrales. Funerary inscriptions provide the largest bulk of epigraphic survivals from the ancient world. This is perhaps not surprising—the less so when we consider what would be the case in the event of the destruction of our own civilisation: the sites of cemeteries in European or American towns and villages would provide a rich source of material for the epigraphists of the time, and might well lead them to false conclusions concerning the virtues of our generation and the piety of the age. The variety in Greek inscribed epitaphs ranges from a simple expression of the name (usually in the nominative, less commonly in the genitive, and occasionally in the dative case, and often accompanied, in the Hellenistic period and later, by the addition of an *envoi*, χαῖρε), to a long account in verse of the life and death of the deceased. Some of these last, especially those connected with children, are often touching in their simplicity or their naïveté: others are realistic to a degree.[8] Long eulogies in prose, such as are not infrequent in seventeenth- and eighteenth-century epitaphs in English churches, did not form part of the Greek tradition of sepulcral inscriptions.

Verse epitaphs are common in the early period, when they are generally content with a line or two; but they continue, with a growing tendency to prolixity, throughout the classical period. They never in fact lost their popularity, although they seldom succeeded in recapturing the simple dignity of the early examples. There are several basic motifs on which they rang the changes: 'here lies...' (ἐνθάδε κεῖται), 'this is the tomb of...' (σῆμα τόδ' ἐστι...), '*A* set up this monument over *B*...', 'I am the tomb of *B*...', etc. Many epitaphs urge the passer-by to stop and read what is inscribed on the stone, and then go on his way a sadder and a wiser man; there are even conversations between the tomb and the inquisitive or reluctant traveller. Many, too, address the bereaved, and urge them not to grieve too much. Stock sentiments include the consolatory 'God taketh soonest those he loveth best' or the pessimistic 'no one can live for ever' (οὐδεὶς ἀθάνατος).

The simplest type names the deceased and no more—sometimes the single name, without further elaboration, sometimes with patronymic and demotic or ethnic, or with one of the two. Of this kind are also the inscriptions accompanying funerary reliefs on stelae or stone *lekythoi*, in which the name serves as a label of identification for the deceased and for any others portrayed in the sculptured group. Where more than one person is named, it is not always clear on such groups which is the figure actually to be regarded as the member of the family who has died. Fourth-century Athens produced a series of such reliefs, in which the sculpture is at times representative of the highest quality in Attic art of the period, while funeral stelae of less complex but (for the period) no less skilful artistry appear in the sixth and fifth centuries also. Expensive reliefs were banned, as far as the Athenians were concerned, by a law of Demetrius of Phalerum during his ten-year régime from 317 to 307 (Cicero, *De Legibus* II, 66), and thereafter commemorative stones are always more modest in size and appearance. Simpler stelae had, of course, existed side by side with the more elaborate forms of funeral monument already described, and, at its very simplest, an epitaph may be no more than a name roughly inscribed on a rock. But the commonest types of monument were the small cylindrical marker (*columella*), seldom more than two feet high, the rectangular *cippus*, or the plain stele with little or no ornamentation. These are inscribed, as mentioned above, with the name of the deceased with or without further description. Sometimes, although hardly at all before the third century, a descriptive adjective is added, of which χρηστός is the most popular, and may occur with or without a χαῖρε.[9] Epitaphs of women sometimes record their father's name and demotic and, if they are married, their husband's name and demotic also. In other parts of Greece the varying customs and attitudes of mind towards death produced local variants: that of describing the dead person as ἥρως is particularly common.

Sometimes the phraseology of the epitaph serves to include the thoughts of the bereaved who have been left behind. The formula μνήμης χάριν or ἕνεκα, while found with a simple epitaph recording the name of the deceased and no more, is also frequent when accompanying a record that *A* set up the tomb over *B*. It is especially common in the Roman period, and recurs with particular frequency in Asia Minor. Also in Asia Minor are found frequent examples of the preparation of a tomb by its future occupant during his lifetime, perhaps on the occasion of the death of one of his young children, large enough to accommodate the whole family as need arises. For unauthorised persons to open such a tomb in order to rifle or re-use it was a major crime against both god and man, and injunctions against this, often with financial penalties prescribed, are not infrequently added. The variations are so numerous that it would hardly be worth while to include too great an assortment of examples; some of the more standard variants have been illustrated at the end of the chapter. But since a knowledge of the parallels that exist, or of what forms are to be expected, in this or that class of inscription governs the epigraphist's ability to identify or restore other fragments of the same type, it is worth the effort on the part of the intending specialist, and it is a matter of course for the specialist *déjà arrivé* to keep a careful note of varieties, of their date, and of their provenience. And the amateur also will find his interest greatly enhanced by a realisation of the richness of theme and variation which the Greeks achieved, especially in their metrical epitaphs, though admittedly laconic single-name tomb-stones belong to the more depressing branches of Greek epigraphy.

Manumissions. The formula of liberation, which reflects the means by which the freeing of a slave was in many instances carried through, is seen here in an example from Delphi (p. 127, below). An impressive series of 'freedom by dedication' manumissions has survived from the site of the great sanctuary, for which the guarantors and *patroni* were people of the locality in Phocis and Locris. Details of the transaction may vary from place to place (cf. *SEG* XII 315, for example, from Macedonia), as with other types of inscriptions, and sometimes the liberation is more briefly expressed, but with the general style and phraseology in mind it is not difficult to identify examples when they occur. Sometimes the manumission was conditional on the freed slave's continued service with the *patronus* or *patrona*, full liberty being acquired only on the death of the latter, and examples are found of other 'strings' being attached (see, for example, *SEG* XIV 529, from Cos). But it is seldom that the 'dedication' meant anything serious, and the device apparently amounted to little more than a legal fiction.[10]

Prosopography. Inscriptions of all types bring us into contact with a great multitude of people, of all walks of life, whose existence is not so much as hinted at in our literary sources, but who, while the central characters of history stand out at the front of the stage more clearly to our view in the glare of the lights, belong to the ranks of the unsung millions who form the crowd at the back. We come into a closer touch with the ordinary man in the street, people of whom we may know only that they died, and therefore that they had lived, people who composed the armies with which the leaders confronted each other, people who cast their vote in the assemblies and went back to their humdrum occu-pations, who did not in themselves make history but who enabled history to be made. We may thus enter more fully into the ancient com-munities and acquire a fairer perspective of them through a greater knowledge of the 'little people' who formed them. Yet inscriptions have in many cases been able also to shed new light on characters well known to the historical tradition, and details of genealogy, even for persons known only through inscriptions, have been filled in on the basis of epigraphic evidence. This prosopographical study is particu-larly valuable for the social historian, but it may have its bearing on a variety of problems, and it is helpful at times in the dating of the inscriptions themselves, as will be described in the next chapter.

The evidence of inscriptions has therefore been one of the firmest bases of those who have compiled *prosopographiae*, or lists of persons known, with the details of passages which give the information about them. The great work of Kirchner, *Prosopographia Attica*, now fifty years old, is in great need of revision in the light of modern epigraphic discoveries, and a card index which records more up-to-date information is now available at the Institute for Advanced Study in Princeton, New Jersey, U.S.A. A prosopography for the Argolid, by M. T. Mitsos, and another for Macedonia by D. Kanatsoules, mark the beginnings of similar coverage for other parts of Greece, and Ptolemaic Egypt is prosopographically served by the *Prosopographia Ptolemaica* of W. Peremans and E. van 't Dack. In addition, the indexes of the *Corpus*, of the *Supplementum Epigraphicum Graecum*, and of other epigraphic publications, offer a constant reminder of the wealth of material that lies ready to hand for the student of prosopography, who may find in it a fresh and stimulating approach to the problems of the ancient world.

This chapter has been able to deal only with a few of the more important types of inscription which those concerned with the subject are, on the whole, most likely to meet. Numerous minor classes remain, some of which have themselves been the subjects of impressive and full-scale studies; a few may perhaps be briefly mentioned: boundary stones recording the limits of a sanctuary, public area, or privately owned property; mortgage stones indicating that such private property has been pledged as security on a dowry or a loan; vase inscriptions recording the owner, painter, or manufacturer of a pot; casual inscriptions, often to indicate ownership, on a variety of small objects; ostraca, the fragments of potsherds used at Athens for the inscribing of the name of the politician against whom the writer wished to vote in the *ostrakophoria*; officials' marks stamped on the handles of amphorae, even the graffiti of tourists on convenient walls to record their visit to the site—an ancient as well as a modern predilection, which is sometimes of considerable value for one branch or another of classical studies. All in all there is a rich treasure-house of material awaiting anyone who cares, as it were, to push the door ajar; and epigraphy is a study which is constantly changing or expanding as new discoveries are made. Here least of all can it be alleged that Greek is a subject with no future. There is, with the study of Greek inscriptions, always a to-morrow to reveal something new, buried or forgotten for some two thousand years, which may confirm or upset the most careful scholarship of yesterday and today.

EXAMPLES

1. A simple preamble, from a decree of the city of Cnidus concerning the sanctuary of Dionysus; third cent. B.C. Dittenberger, *Sylloge*³ 978.

> "Εδοξε Κνιδίοι[ς,γν]-
> ὦμα προστατᾶ[ν]·
> περὶ ὧν τοὶ Βάκ[χοι]
> ἐπῆλθον, ὅπω[ς] κτλ.

2. An Attic preamble of the mid-fourth century, from a decree in honour of Theogenes of Naucratis. *IG* ii² 206, ll. 1–8.

> 'Επὶ τῆς Πανδιονίδος ἐνάτης π[ρυτα]-
> νείας ἧι Διεύχης Δημάρχου Φρε[άρρ]-
> ιος ἐγραμμάτευεν. Σωκέρδης 'Αλ[αιε]-
> ὺς ἐπεστάτει· Καλλίμαχος ἦρχεν· [ἔδ]-
> 5   οξεν τῆι βουλῆι καὶ τῶι δήμωι· 'Ιε[ρο]-
> κλείδης Τιμοστράτου 'Αλωπεκῆθε[ν]
> εἶπεν· ἐπειδὴ Θεογένης ὁ Ναυκρατί-
> της ἀνὴρ ἀγαθός ἐστιν κτλ.

3. A decree from Delphi, of the last part of the fourth century, in the simplest of terms, granting privileges in consultation of the oracle to the Corcyraeans. *SEG* XII 229.

> Θεός· τύχαι ἀγαθᾶι·   5   τος Μαιμάλου, βου-
> Δελφοὶ ἔδωκαν Κορ-   λευόντων Μένητος,
> κυραίοις προμαντεί-   [Κ]λεοβούλου.
> [α]ν,προεδρίαν· ἀρχον-

4. Record of expenditure. The first lines of the record of loans from the Sacred Treasuries to the Athenian state, 426–425 B.C. *IG* I² 324.

> [Τάδε ἐλογίσαν]το ℎοι λογιστα[ὶ ἐν τοῖς τέτ]ταρσιν ἔτεσιν ἐκ
> Παναθεναίον ἐς [Παναθέναια ὀφειλ]-
> [όμενα. τάδε ℎο]ι ταμίαι παρέδοσ[αν 'Ανδρο]κλῆς Φλυεὺς καὶ χσυνάρχοντες
> ℎελλ[ενοταμίαις.....]
> ....ει καὶ χσυνάρχοσι[ν στρατ]εγοῖς ℎιπποκράτει Χολαργεῖ καὶ
> χου[νάρχοσιν ἐπὶ τῆς]
> [Κεκροπίδο]ς πρυτανείας δευτέ[ρας πρυ]τανευόσες, κτλ.

5. *Traditio rerum sacrarum*. A preamble of the early fourth century. *IG* ii² 1378.

> [Τάδε παρέδοσαν οἱ ταμίαι τῶν ἱ]ερῶγ χρημάτων
> [τῆς 'Αθηνάας καὶ τῶν ἄλλων θεῶν] οἱ ἐπὶ 'Αριστοκ-
> [ράτος ἄρχοντος Σωκράτης Λα]μπτρεύς, ν Φίλιπ-
> [πος...¹²........, ν ....δωρος *Ο]αθε[ν], ν Θωρυκί[ω]-
> 5   [ν ...⁷...ης, ν Δίων ...⁷..., ν] Λαμπροκλῆς Φλ-

[υεύς, ν 'Επικράτης ....⁸.....]s, Δημοκράτης ν

['Ραμνόσιος, ν ....¹¹...... Αἰγι]λιεύς, ν οἶς Χαι-

[ρίων 'Ελευσίνιος ἐγραμμάτευε], vacat

[παραδεξάμενοι παρὰ τῶν προτέρ]ων τα[μ]ιῶν τῶν

10 [ἐπὶ Λάχητος ἄρχοντος Μείδωνο]ς Ε[ὐ]ωνυμέως κα-

[ὶ ξυναρχόντων, ν οἶς Θερσίλοχο]ς Οἰναῖος ἐγρα-

[μμάτευε, ν ἀριθμῶι καὶ σταθμῶι] ἐκ τõ 'Οπισθοδό-

[μο· κτλ.]

6. Dedication. Name of the god only. From Ceus, first cent. A.D. (?)
SEG XIV 536.
'Ερμῆι καὶ 'Ηρακ[λεῖ].

7. Dedication to a Roman Emperor. From Athens, c. A.D. 132. SEG XII
148.
[Αὐτοκ]ράτο-
[ρι Καί]σαρι Τραϊα-
νῷ 'Αδριανῷ
κτίστῃ 'Ολυ[μ]-
5   πίῳ.

8. Dedication with the name in the genitive case. From Delos, second or
first century B.C. SEG XIII 424.
['Αφρ]οδίτης.

9. Dedication including the formula 'sacred to'. From Paestum, sixth
century B.C. SEG XII 412.
Τᾶς ἥρας ἱαρόν.

10. Dedication with formula 'I belong to'. From Argos, fifth century
B.C. IG IV 566.
Τοῖ Ϝανάκοι: ἐμί: Εὔδ[ικο]ς: ἀνέθεκε.

11. Fuller form of dedication, with artist's signature added. From Her-
mione, fifth century B.C. IG IV 683.
'Αλεξίας Λύονος ἀνέθε[κε]
τᾶι Δάματρι: τᾶι Χθονία[ι]
ἑρμιονεύς.
Κρεσίλας ἐποίεσε Κυδονιάτ[ας].

12. Honours paid to a proconsul's wife by the city of Caunus, A.D. 33/4.
SEG XIV 646.
'Ο δῆμος ὁ Καυνίων ἐπαινεῖ
καὶ στεφανοῖ χρυσέωι στεφάνωι,
τειμᾷ δὲ καὶ εἰκόνι χαλκῇ,
Πλαυτίαν Αὔλου θυγατέρα,
5   γυναῖκα δὲ Ποπλίου Πετρωνίου
τὸ πέμπτον ἀνθυπάτου.

13. Statue base, with verb omitted, honouring Octavianus Caesar, 31–27 B.C. From Ceus. *SEG* XIV 537.

Ὁ δῆμος
Αὐτοκράτορα Καίσαρα θεὸν
θεοῦ ὑόν.

14. Similar base, from Athens, honouring Herod the Great, and adding the reasons for the honour. 27–4 B.C. *SEG* XII 150.

['Ο δῆμος]
[βασιλέα Ἡρώδην Εὐ]σεβῆ καὶ
[Φιλοκαίσαρα ἀρετῆς] ἕνεκα
[καὶ εὐεργεσί]ας.

15. Funerary *columella*, giving name of the deceased only. Roman period, from Athens. *IG* II² 11979.

Λυκάων.

16. Similar *columella*, with greeting added. First century B.C., from Athens. *IG* II² 10920.

Ἀφροδισία | χαῖρε.

17. Similar *columella*, with epithet added. Roman period, from Athens. *IG* II² 10918.

Ἀφροδισία | χρηστή.

18. Funerary stele, showing name and patronymic. End of fourth century B.C., from Athens. *SEG* XII 208.

Ἱέρων | Ἱερωνύμου.

19. Similar stele, showing name and demotic. Early fourth century B.C., from Athens. *IG* II² 6415.

Εὐθύδημος | Κηφισιεύς.

20. Funerary *columella*, showing name and ethnic. First century A.D., from Eleusis. *IG* II² 10259; *SEG* XIV 224.

Ζώπυρ[ος] | Σερίφιος.

21. Similar *columella*, showing name, patronymic, and demotic. Middle of the second century A.D., from Athens. *SEG* XII 181.

Ἀφροδείσιος | Φιλοστράτου | Ῥαμνούσιος.

22. Similar *columella*, showing name, patronymic, and ethnic. Third century B.C., from Athens. *SEG* XII 188.

Σφαῖρος | Σφαίρου | Ἀντιοχεύς.

23. Funerary monument of a woman, showing names of father and husband. First century A.D., from Athens. *IG* II² 9712; *SEG* XIII 160.

Εἰσικ[ράτεια] | Θεοδ[ώρου] | Μιλ[ησία], | Σωπ[άτρου] || [γυνή].

IV. CLASSIFICATION OF INSCRIPTIONS

24. Epitaph of a woman, combining several features. Roman period, from Caria. *SEG* xiv 701.

Εὐφραντίς, γυνὰ δὲ
Διογένευς, χρηστὰ
χαῖρε.

25. Epitaph containing penalties for violation of the tomb. Roman period, from Caria. *SEG* xiv 659(*b*).

[Μ. Αὐρ]η(λίου) 'Επιγόνου τάφος·
[μετὰ δὲ] τὴν τελευτή (*sic*) μου μηδένα ἐξὸν εἶναι
[τεθῆνα]ι εἰ μὴ τὴν σύνβιόν μου 'Αρτεμεισίαν
[κὲ 'Επίγο]νον τὸν υεἱόν μου· αἰὰν δέ τις μετὰ τοὺς
5   [γεγραμμ]ένους βιάσητ *ννν* αι *vacat*
θεῖναι, δώσι | τῇ πόλει | (δηνάρια) φ'.

26. Funerary stele, with the formula μνείας χάριν. Roman period, from Beroea in Macedonia. *SEG* xii 328.

5   Κλεαγόρα Βότ|ρυϊ τῷ υἱῷ ἐκ | τῶν ἰδίων μνεί|ας χάριν· χαῖ||ρε,
παροδεῖτα.

27. Funerary monument, with a variation of the same formula. Roman period, from Caria. *SEG* xii 444.

'Ιατρικῆς τῆς | 'Ερμοῦ μνή|μης χάριν.

28. Mark of ownership. Graffito on the foot of a *kylix*, found at Old Smyrna. Seventh century B.C. *SEG* xii 480.

Δολίωνός ἐμι φυλίχνη.

29. Similar graffito, from Camirus, Rhodes. Fifth century B.C. *IG* xii
1,719.
Φιλτός ἤμι τᾶς καλᾶς ἁ κύλιχς ἁ ποικίλα.

51

CHAPTER V

THE DATING OF INSCRIPTIONS

AN inscription may be of interest by reason of the language in which it is expressed, or in the historical or social application of its contents, or in some other way or combination of ways, but, whatever the field of study for which it may provide useful material, it loses a very great part of its value if it cannot be dated and set into some sort of chronological context.[1] In many cases, even in the majority of cases, a precise dating is impossible, and it would be misleading to attempt to offer one. In this event, the most that can be done is to suggest the period within which, as it appears, the inscription may be safely attributed—'the Hellenistic period', 'aetas Imperii Romani', or, more closely, the second century B.C., the first century A.D., and so forth. In the editing of an inscription some indication of date ought always to be given, even though it be of the vaguest. It is to be regretted that instances still recur of the reporting or editing of inscriptions in which the finder or editor fails to make even the most non-committal suggestion of the period to which it is to be assigned. More frequently, perhaps, the editor may leave the reader to deduce such attribution for himself from the photograph or drawing provided. But to make the attribution is the province of the editor, not of the reader, who may indeed lack the epigraphic skill and intimate knowledge of the subject or region in question to be able to make it with confidence. However, most publications of texts do usually contain information about the dating of the inscriptions with which they are concerned.

A scholar or student who is not himself a specialist in epigraphy may well, on digesting the information, rest content to accept what the 'professional' epigraphist has told him, and he is generally justified in so doing. But it may be that he feels sceptical of what he reads, and yet is doubtful of his own qualifications to pursue an independent line of thought. On what basis can he set about having his own opinions on such a matter? How, for example, are we to set a date not only to a decree which announces its own date in so many words but to a half-obliterated dedication or a fragmentary two-line epitaph? There are, indeed, a number of criteria which may prove of use in providing the answers. Some of them offer more certainty in their application than others; some of them, for a variety of reasons, prove inapplicable in a great number of cases. But by bearing them in mind, and with increasing experience in their use, it is possible to provide oneself with a tolerably firm basis for an independent judgement on epigraphic dating.

1. *The provenience of the inscription.* Although some ancient sites, such as Athens, had a continuous history throughout the period of classical antiquity, there are many which did not, and the destruction or foundation of these provides convenient *termini ante* or *post quem* which eliminate some of the wider dating possibilities. For instance, an inscription from Olynthus in the Chalcidic peninsula is likely to ante-date the destruction of the city by Philip II of Macedon in 348–347 B.C. A decree passed by the people of the city of Stratonicea in Caria could hardly be dated earlier than the period in the third century B.C. (about the year 265) when it was founded.[2] There may be a re-foundation of a city on a site which had been earlier destroyed, as happened at Corinth, and in this case inscriptions are unlikely to be datable to the inter-vening period when the ravaged site remained unoccupied. Finally, there may have been an interval during which, for economic or other reasons, a state was in a period of eclipse, when its ability to set up epigraphic records was limited, or when it was unable to act *suo iure*; or, as in classical Sparta, there may have been circumstances in which a fully developed and flourishing community simply was not in the habit of committing records to stone.

As a qualification of this point, it may be noted that isolated settle-ments may continue to exist on abandoned sites, and these may leave casual records such as grave monuments. The complete absence of all epigraphic remains after such a *terminus ante quem* is therefore not to be regarded as a necessary supposition, but such remains by their very poverty generally emphasise the break which has taken place.

Even within a city area or otherwise limited site, the actual archaeo-logical provenience may provide a *terminus* of some sort or another. At Athens, inscriptions built into the Themistoclean wall or found with other debris buried on the Acropolis after the sack of the city by the Persians are presumably to be dated before 480 B.C., or they would not have been available for the purpose to which they were put, or found in the context in which they were. Similarly, inscriptions built into the so-called Valerian wall may be presumed to antedate A.D. 267, the date of the sack by the invading Herulians, in consequence of which the new defensive wall was hurriedly built. At Olympia, a long base containing three important dedications[3] underlay a part of the foundations of the great mid-fifth century temple of Zeus; from their archaeological context these dedications must be given a date earlier than that of the temple. Furthermore, dates won by these means may reflect on the dating of other documents, perhaps in themselves without a firm date, on which they throw light by reason of their content, or with which comparative study is able to bring them into relationship.

2. *The character of the monument.* This criterion may vary from the simple to the highly complex. In its simplest form we may put it that an inscription on an Attic 'Little Master' cup, painted on the vase before it was fired, will belong to the date or period to which such cups are to be assigned. It was mentioned in an earlier chapter that at Athens expensive grave reliefs, some of which almost amounted to complete statuary groups, were banned not later than 312 B.C. Inscriptions found on such a monument, or which, even if the statues themselves have perished, clearly belong to one, ought as a result to be dated no later than 312.

More complex are the archaeological criteria introduced from other branches of the study. The date of the introduction of an architectural, sculptural, or other artistic technique or motif is likely to have some bearing on the date of any inscription which may be associated with the object or monument on which it is found. It is necessary, in these cases, to beware of circular arguments. Scholars concerned with architectural, sculptural or other problems may sometimes ask the epigraphist's help, and try to date their motifs by calling in the dating of the accompanying inscription: it then becomes easy to reverse the process and date the inscription by the architecture or sculpture.

Artistic criteria of this type may be reinforced by historical considerations. For example, an inscription concerning the cult of Mithras may be dated with the assistance of the knowledge of the period during which the Mithraic cult flourished; but it may also be dated by the style and characteristics of the sculptured group of Mithras Tauroctonus which may accompany it, or by some iconographic feature to which those expert in the development of Mithraism may be able to assign a relatively precise date; and finally, there will be the testimony of the actual archaeological context in which it was originally unearthed.

To these first two criteria-headings, therefore, the archaeological and artistic data form an essential background. The skilled epigraphist must of necessity be something of an archaeologist and something of a historian. It is impossible to study an inscription *in vacuo*, so to speak, without reference to one or both of these major fields of study, and experience in both of them is desirable as a preparation for specialisation in epigraphy itself. An epigraphist must be able to draw on wide resources; unless he restricts himself to a narrow field, he may be faced, even on a single site, with material which covers the whole length of classical antiquity, and the variety of the content of his epigraphic finds, which we have glanced at in the previous chapter, shows that he must be equipped to deal with a great diversity of subjects and problems.

Unfortunately many inscriptions have reached the museums unaccompanied by any artistic attachment and without any record of their origin, let alone their precise archaeological context. They may have been bought on the open market, in some centre such as Smyrna, to which antiquities found in the neighbourhood used at one time to gravitate for sale. This is the origin of much of the interesting collection of inscriptions from Asia Minor which, purchased by various private collectors, is now at the museum of the University of Leiden. Or inscriptions may simply be discovered on, and correctly noted as coming from, a site which is in fact different from their original location.[4] Stones may, in one way or another, travel considerable distances, and not necessarily for the purpose of being housed in a museum. This happens not uncommonly in Asia Minor, but not only there. For example, some inscriptions from Megara, listed in *IG* VII, have found their way to Athens or Aegina; the possibility remains that fragments in Athens, not otherwise identifiable, may have been brought from Megara and therefore be more properly assigned to *IG* VII rather than *IG* II². In many cases the origin of the stone has to be deduced from the contents of the inscription itself[5] and from others that may be compared with it. But, even in the best regulated and documented collection of inscriptions, there generally remains a residue of '*Tituli originis incertae*'.

3. *The content of the inscription.* Much trouble may of course be saved, and a comparatively close, perhaps even exact, dating obtained, if the inscription on the stone betrays its own date in the course of its contents. It may do this in a variety of ways, some explicit and precise, some less so, and it is probably more useful to consider some of these under individual headings.

(i) *Connexion with a known historical theme or a known historical event.* At its simplest, this may prove to be no more than an indication in general terms such as that suggested above in dealing with a Mithraic monument: the *floruit* of such an inscription is known to be limited, and other examples of the same type may therefore be set within the same limits. But it may be that an inscription contains a direct reference to some matter or event well known in the literary tradition or securely dated from other sources; in that case the attribution of the inscription to a corresponding date can be made with some measure of safety. Take for instance the helmet which Hiero, tyrant of Syracuse, dedicated at Olympia as part of the spoils of his victory over the Etruscans—'spoils from Cumae', as the inscription reads.[6] This battle is known to us from Pindar and from Diodorus Siculus, and may be dated with confidence in 474 B.C. The dedication was, we may presume, inscribed shortly after the event.

(ii) *Connexion with a known historical person and his activities.* This may narrow the dating possibilities considerably. As a simple example, a fragment, otherwise undated, but with enough remaining to suggest that it was a decree proposed by the orator Demades, must be assigned to the time at which Demades was proposing decrees. It may even be that we are well enough informed about the character concerned to be able to suggest that an inscription referring to him must be connected with a particular period of his career. There is a Delphian decree[7] in honour of Aristotle the philosopher and of his nephew Callisthenes. This decree certainly postdates 339 B.C., since it contains a reference to 'treasurers' who are known to have been first instituted then. We also know that these treasurers paid for the inscribing of the list of Pythian victors, for the compilation of which Aristotle and Callisthenes were honoured, in the archonship of Caphis, 327–6. Callisthenes died in 327 while accompanying the expedition of Alexander the Great, on which he had departed in 334; the decree in his honour must fall between 339 and 327, possibly quite close to the latter date.

(iii) *Other prosopographical indications.* The importance of inscriptions for prosopographical studies has already been emphasised.[8] A study of the names and patronymics appearing on inscriptions, whether of persons mentioned in historical sources or those for whom epigraphy provides the sole evidence, may sometimes be helpful in the determination of date. Again, this may be a simple deduction, such as that a grave inscription showing the deceased as from the deme Berenikidai cannot be dated earlier than the institution of the deme in the later third century. But one may take into account more complex details: correspondences among patronymics and demotics, cross-references concerning offices held or *res gestae* in general, family connexions expressed particularly on funerary inscriptions, the frequent custom of preserving the same names in a family and of naming one's son after his grandfather. The information from Attic sources is particularly rich, and this method can be used for Athenian families with great effect: reliance on it will undoubtedly prove of the highest value in the compilation of a new *Prosopographia Attica*. By co-ordinating all the various features mentioned, it becomes possible at times to construct genealogical tables for the families recorded, and these, by a rough assessment of years per generation, may offer a date for an inscription to which such evidence can be referred. Although the completeness of the data makes the approach particularly applicable to Athens, it, or methods of comparison along much the same lines, has been and will be found no less helpful at any site where the epigraphic harvest has been substantial.

(iv) *Dating by the calendar*.[9] Sometimes an inscription provides its own date by incorporating a record of the day, month and year on which the decree it records was passed, or the list was drawn up, or the person there commemorated died. In this last instance, that of epitaphs, the inclusion of a date is a feature of the imperial period, and more specifically of Christian tombstones, but is not without examples in Hellenistic times; its expression may vary according to the inscription's provenience. Casual graffiti also sometimes include a date. But most important are those which appear in the preamble or epilogue of an official document. In the Attic examples of the fourth century and later, which are probably the most comprehensive, the date is recorded on the basis both of the day and month according to the lunar calendar and of the name of the tribe 'in prytany', its number in the series, and the number of days it has been in office. The names of the lunar months differed from city to city, although most of them were based on the names of deities and festivals some of which recur in various places in the same or similar forms, these being the gods or celebrations with which the month in question was particularly connected. However, the same name in different cities may well not refer to the same period of the year. Lunar months varied between 29 and 30 days, and extra months or days were from time to time intercalated when it became necessary to correct discrepancies between the lunar and solar calendars. Intercalation, or sometimes retardation, of the calendar might also be made for political rather than astronomical reasons.[10]

It is in the designation of the year that the main difficulties arise. Sometimes the year is quoted as a number. This number may be based on an 'era', such as that familiar from the Roman reckoning *ab urbe condita* (which is, however, epigraphically rare), associated with the city or region in question. These eras changed from time to time, according to the political vicissitudes which the locality experienced. Under the settled conditions of the Roman Empire, an era based on the date of the battle of Actium was widespread in the Greek-speaking parts of Europe. In other cases it was the formation of the area into a Roman province which gave the starting-point for the reckoning; Syria counted from its pacification by Pompey in 63 B.C., Galatia from 25 B.C., the death of its last king, Amyntas, and its incorporation into the area of direct Roman rule. Some manœuvring of the calendar might also prove a useful honorific device. Such was, for instance, the origin of the months July and August, while the inhabitants of the province of Asia reorganised their official year as a compliment to Augustus, to make it begin on his birthday.[11]

An official numerical designation for the year was slow to be introduced, and was not in existence at all until the Hellenistic period. The customary method of naming the year in the ordinary city-state was with reference to the year of office of a priest or magistrate. The unsatisfactoriness of this method, for his purposes, was keenly felt by Thucydides, who gave the date of the outbreak of the Peloponnesian War with a cumbersome reference to the Athenian archon, the Spartan ephors, and the priestess of Hera at Argos, but who otherwise preferred a system of his own which reckoned by seasons, summers and winters. The reckoning of years in terms of the quadrennial celebrations of the Olympic games, popular in literature, was another attempt to find some universal term of reference which stepped beyond the confines of the individual *polis*. But officially the eponymous magistracy or priesthood gave the year its name; it was the year of the priesthood of x or the archonship of y. The information is helpful to us in so far as we know, in the terms of the Julian calendar, when the priest or magistrate named held his office. Unfortunately this is not always, or even often, the case —even in Athens, where, as will be described in Chapter x, the archonlist of the third and later centuries continues to be a subject of dispute and of constant revision. It is also essential to know when the year of office of the eponymous official began. At Athens the archon took office at the beginning of the month Hekatombaion, roughly in early July, so that years derived from an archon's name must always be designated in our terms with a double date, since they fall half in one Julian year and half in another, e.g. 427/6 B.C. If a month is mentioned on the inscription in association with the archonship, e.g. the second prytany, it becomes possible to give a more exact date such as 427/6 B.C., or August/September 427.

Uncertain as our knowledge is for Athens, other than in the fifth and fourth centuries, we are in worse case with the eponymous officials of other cities. Where material is fairly extensive it has proved possible to construct a list of magistrates which fixes their dates within narrow limits, and this has been done with conspicuous success, in the case of the Delphic material, by G. Daux in his *Chronologie delphique*, while enough data may exist to establish at least some fixed points in other areas, as for example in the list of Aetolian *strategoi*. But even where actual lists of magistrates survive, as at Tauromenium in Sicily (*IG* XIV 421–2), it may not be possible to fix their beginning and their end in terms of years B.C. and A.D., even though they do provide comparative dates, in their own terms, for the magistrates named. The title of the eponymous magistrate or priest varied from place to place. In Asia Minor it is the *stephanephoros* who is most frequently met with as the magistrate who gave his name to the year; in classical Sparta it was the ephor, although the same city in the imperial period reckoned by *patronomoi*. As offices became, in the course of time, more of a burden than an honour, it became not unusual for a god to be designated eponymous magistrate, the financial contributions associated with the office being paid from the temple treasury. Since the same god might fill the same office on a number of occasions, this made for even greater difficulty in using the name as a calendaric reference, and the same was true when, over a long period of time, several men with the same name held the eponymous office. In such cases, the reference would be enlarged by including also the name of the preceding office-holder— 'the year of *x*, who came after *y*'.

(v) *The regnal year of a king or emperor*. A year expressed as a number may bear reference not to a city or provincial era but to the reign of the current king or Roman emperor, the number being given in terms of the year of his supremacy, ἔτους *x*. The name of the king is usually given, which makes the translation into our own terms a simple matter, provided that we know the point at which the king in question came to the throne or at any rate from which he counted his regnal years. Conversely, an inscription datable on other grounds, which also happens to carry a regnal date, may help to clear up a disputed point of this kind regarding the royal history (see for instance *SEG* XII 373). Under the Roman Empire the system which had obtained under the Hellenistic kings continued, with the substitution of the emperor for the Syrian, Egyptian or other monarch; this was particularly so in Egypt, with the added complication that the identity of the emperor may not be specified and so may remain unclear. The word ἔτους, in inscriptions as in papyri, is often abbreviated to ∟ .

In city inscriptions, the regnal date, if given, is usually associated with a date reckoned according to local custom, since under the Hellenistic monarchies and under the rule of Rome the cities were tenacious of their individuality and such semblance of real independence as they possessed. Documents such as royal letters and rescripts, which cannot be tied to any local calendar, had no means of showing a date other than that of the year of the king from whose court they emanated, but this had the advantage that it would be readily intelligible in all parts of the kingdom.

4. *The type of the inscription, and the methods of expression and formulas used.* It may prove that neither the archaeological data nor the matters discussed nor the people mentioned in an inscription yield the required information, and the problem of setting a date to it remains. Some help towards a date of reasonable accuracy may in that case be sought simply from a consideration of the type of inscription it seems to be, and by looking at *how* it says what it says. Inscriptions of a certain character may belong only to a limited period of time. For example, it so happens that all the documents found at Athens which relate to the leasing of the silver mines at Laurium fall within the years 367–307 B.C.[12] This may be no more than a coincidence, but it creates a supposition that any documents of the same character which may be found in the future are likely to be datable within the same limits. Ephebic inscriptions are not found in Athens before 332 B.C., and mostly belong to the Hellenistic and Roman periods, when the institution flourished and was a particular source of Athenian pride; new finds will, in all probability, fall into line with what is already known. *Stoichedon* texts, as noted in Chapter III, are rarely met with after 225 B.C. or thereabouts, and any new discovery is likely to be attributable to some date earlier than that.

Such *termini ante* or *post quem* may also be helped by historical data or by prosopographical indications as outlined in 3, iii, above. Inscriptions containing an abundance of Aurelius names appear, *prima facie* at least, to postdate A.D. 212 and the citizenship edict of the emperor Aurelius Caracalla. More accurately, obvious *liberti* or their descendants, who bear the name Ulpius, are unlikely to appear on inscriptions of a date earlier than the reign of Trajan. The loss of Athenian naval power after 322 B.C. makes it unlikely that any fragments of naval records found in Athens or the Piraeus hereafter should be dated later than that year. Indeed, the whole decline of Athens as a great power suggests that inscriptions showing strong Athenian activity in international affairs as a power to be reckoned with should be of an earlier rather than a later date. Athenian epigraphic remains do in fact show a shift of emphasis, after the Macedonian conquest, from treaties and documents associated with public wealth and a vigorous public policy, to a greater concentration on honorary decrees as a means of foreign policy and on the quiet and efficient business of running the domestic affairs of Athens itself.

The terms in which an inscription is couched may also help. As time went on, for instance, decrees tended to become more verbose, and honorary decrees in particular more fulsome, and the phraseology employed became somewhat stereotyped. A study of the development of the language and of the forms of expression used in the different types of document makes it possible to assign new finds at least to their general period if not to any more hard and fast date. Particularly helpful in this connexion are the changes which took place in the well-known formulas which tend to be repeated, in a more or less set form, in inscriptions of the same kind. This is especially true of the preamble of decrees and other public documents, the form of which varied as the procedure in the sovereign body was adapted and modified. To take a familiar instance, the procedure of the ecclesia at Athens was altered in the first quarter of the fourth century (see *SEG* XIV 43), and its chairman was thenceforward no longer the *epistates* but became a syndicated office held by a board of *proedroi*, one of whom put the matter under discussion to the vote. A mention of the *proedroi* in the preamble to a decree would, as a result, not permit the decree in question to be dated earlier than the restoration of the democracy in 403 B.C., and possibly not earlier than 378 B.C., which is the date at which the new function of the *proedroi* first becomes well attested. A change of preamble to include mention of the *symproedroi* puts a document down to 320 B.C. or thereabouts at the earliest. A calendaric date quoting lunar as well as prytany month would suggest a date not earlier than 350 B.C. for the inscription that contained it.

Equally useful is the development in the types of honours and rewards bestowed on benefactors of the state. These begin, in the early period, by being impressive but comparatively modest: thanks, the titles of *proxenos* and *euergetes*, promises of special care, in case of need, by the ecclesia and the executive. Later the expressions of gratitude become more sonorous and the tangible rewards more lavish: statues and crowns, sometimes of gold, were the necessary offerings for the potentates of the Hellenistic period, and liberality to them, or to those advisers and courtiers who were in their confidence, was a wise feature of city-state diplomacy and a sensible measure of self-insurance. It is to that epoch, and to the Roman period (at any rate while cities were still in a position to afford the expense), that such phraseology as that in example 12 on p. 49 above belongs.

Finally, it may be worth while to mention briefly two further instances of development in an inscriptional type which may assist in the dating of other material of the same kind. The general type of the ephebic inscription at Athens is now well enough known for the pattern of its development to be accurately worked out, and for new lists to be set within their proper group;[13] while fashions in sepulchral formulas, the use of phraseology such as ζῶν καὶ φρονῶν or χαῖρε already known from datable material from the same region, often the fulsomeness of expression of the epitaph itself—all these can be at least indicative of the period to which a funerary inscription may, at least on a plausible hypothesis, be ascribed.[14]

5. *The style of lettering and the forms of the letters.* It may be that, notwithstanding all the criteria already mentioned, an inscription is too fragmentary or otherwise too uncommunicative for any conclusions to be safely drawn as the result of applying them; or, since it is desirable to have the support of as many methods of checking as possible, additional support may be needed for a proposed date from some other source; or, lastly, the inscription may be of such a stock, frequently encountered type that it lacks the possibility of being attributed to a reasonable date along the lines suggested. It is at that point that one must turn to the best remaining clue available, the character and style of the writing, and the shapes of the individual letters which go to make up the inscription, along with the technique of the workman who engraved them. Fashions in letter-forms are commonly used as a means to dating. Such statements as 'the lettering indicates a date towards the end of the second century B.C.' or 'first century A.D., on the letter-forms' are familiar in epigraphic publications. But this criterion, so often used as a first resort, is much better left as a final refuge; its evidence is far less precise and secure than is popularly supposed.

It is at its most valuable in the early period, in the seventh, sixth and fifth centuries, when the continual and rapid development of the epichoric alphabets and their gradual assimilation to an Ionic *koine*, as described in Chapter II, make it possible to suggest, on the basis of the appearance of the letters alone, a date sometimes within a decade or two. This is especially true of Attica, where the material is sufficiently abundant and well-known to allow a reasonably close dating on this basis. But it must be admitted that some scholars have overworked what has been called 'intuitive decadology'. Analysis of letter-forms will always rest in some degree upon subjective interpretation, nor can artistic development always be pigeon-holed neatly within this decade or that. Allowance must also be made not only for the style-criticism of the scholar but for the artistic *penchants* of the stone-cutter himself, for his tenacious conservatism or his brave *avant-gardisme*. An old workman, as was remarked in Chapter III, may preserve forms characteristic of earlier decades to a date later than one might, in general, have expected to find them.

By the end of the fifth century the letters and the technique of writing them had completed their necessary development. The epigraphic productions of the time, as Pl. 2 illustrates, not only showed the letters in the fundamental forms which they were to preserve thereafter throughout antiquity, but exemplified the artistic qualities of the stonecutters' work at their classical best. They could not write better, but it was open to them to write differently. What remained concerned fashion and style, with constantly developing variations on the canonical forms. The introduction of new letter-forms may be dated, in a general way, on the basis of inscriptions showing the new forms which are themselves datable on other grounds. This helps to provide a *terminus post quem* which may prove useful in other cases in which no additional criterion will serve to suggest a date. There is, however, seldom a *terminus ante quem*. Styles once introduced tend to persist, side by side with both earlier and later fashions. The classical style of the fourth century B.C. was never wholly eclipsed, even though the decorated and baroque styles of the Hellenistic period exceeded it for a while in general popularity, and it had, as will be described in Chapter VIII, a marked revival in the classicising movement of the time of Trajan and Hadrian. Monumental inscriptions on buildings or imposing statue-groups and memorials often favoured a purity and simplicity of style at a time when monuments of lesser moment rioted in a profusion of exotic by-forms and a tedious abundance of apices. Thus it has proved possible for the most eminent epigraphic authorities to be widely at variance on the date of a text as assessed by the forms of its letters. *SEG* XIII 521, the record of the law governing the duties of the *astynomoi* of the city of Pergamum, has been held, on grounds which are understandable and reasonable on both sides, to belong either to the period of the Pergamene kings, of whom the last died in 133 B.C., or to the reign of Trajan or Hadrian—a discrepancy of two hundred years and more. Either dating would, in fact, not do an injustice to the lettering.

Another point to remember is that a style is not everywhere uniform and contemporaneous.[15] A fashion in one part of the Greek world does not necessarily permit a text from elsewhere, showing similar characteristics in its lettering, to be assigned to the same period. It is, for instance, noticeable that, while from the sixth to the fourth century it may be said that the Attic inscriptional style was the most advanced in all Hellas in the development and execution of its lettering, this ceased to be so after Athens' loss of political importance. There came a conservatism in style and frequently a poverty in execution at a time when particularly fine work was being produced elsewhere—a reflexion perhaps of Athenian reliance on memories of a past greatness to brighten their less significant present. On the whole the most modern trends and the best examples of calligraphic quality are at that time to be found in the city-states of Asia under the great successor-kingdoms. Similarly, even within a single city the type and expensiveness and prominence of the inscription must be borne in mind. Cheap little tombstones or homely dedications may be roughly inscribed, and noted down by the epigraphist as 'pessime inscripti', in all ages. It is easily possible to be betrayed into giving these too archaic a date, or putting them among material of a later period, simply because they are rough and slipshod, or because they incorporate some letter-forms current in popular and cursive writing but not ordinarily used for epigraphic purposes.

Nevertheless, it is possible to make a few suggestions as to the kind of point for which to look: they may perhaps prove helpful, if they are taken as guides in general terms and are not converted into hard and fast rules. With this proviso, and with the expectation that exceptions to all the statements which follow will occur, it may be regarded as generally true, for example, that *alpha* with a broken cross-bar (Λ) is not met with before the third century B.C., and that apices or serifs hardly occur before that time. The beginnings of these, in the slight widening, with a twist of the chisel, of the free ends of the letter-strokes, may indeed be seen both in Athens and elsewhere as early as the 330's (see Chapter VIII below), but they seem to lose their popularity in the Roman period and may be thought of as predominantly a Hellenistic feature. During that period their popularity and variety were considerable, and for these three centuries they have a distinct and useful dating value. ξ and M become Σ and M during the third and second centuries, and the older forms, although not immediately dying out, gradually disappear. Similarly Ξ replaced ₮ during the third century, and Π took the place of Γ somewhat later, in the course of the first centuries B.C. and A.D. But survivals of these older types cannot be excluded at later dates. In the Roman period there may be noticed a growing fondness for elongated forms (Λ for A, Δ for Δ, Λ for Λ, and so forth), as well as for rounded letters (Є, M, C, Ѡ), based on forms used in the cursive script.[16] Illogically, these last were sometimes adapted to the more intractable medium of the stone-cut inscription in a squared form, such as Ϲ and Ш. But a rounded or lunate

PLATE I. An Athenian decree regulating the affairs of
Miletus, 450–449 B.C.

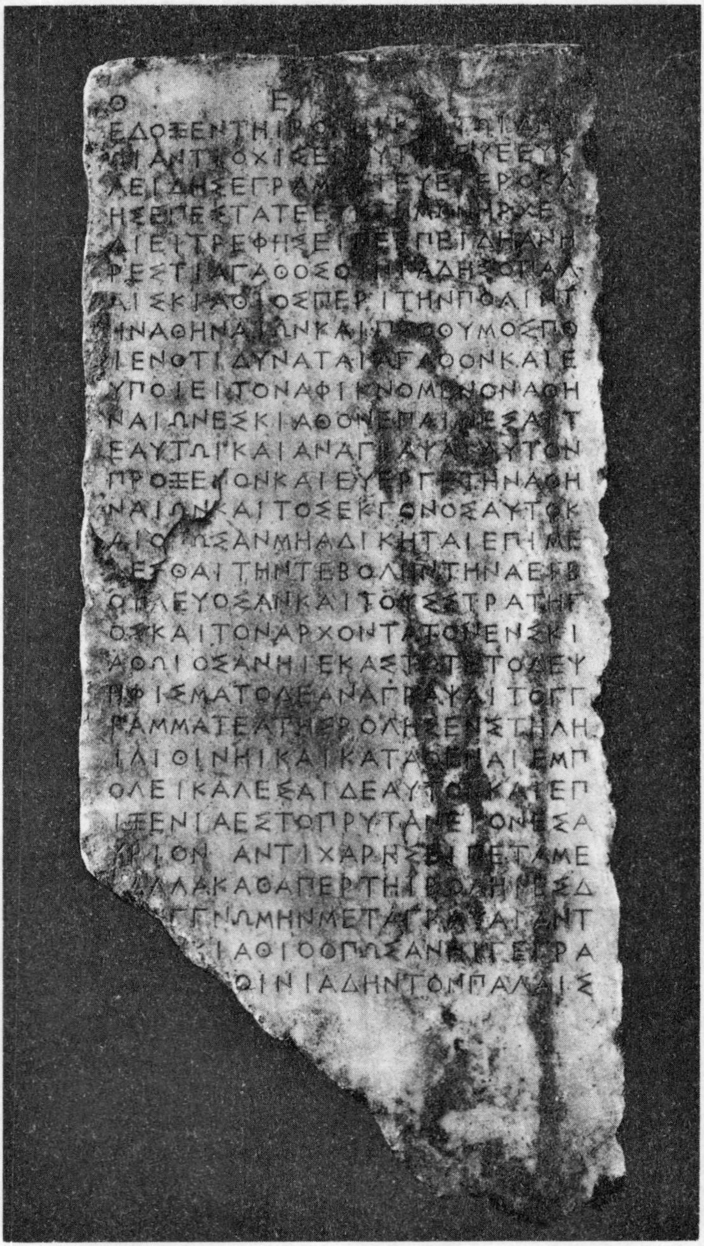

D. A. I. Foto, Athens.

PLATE 2. Athenian decree in honour of Oeniades of Sciathus, 408–407 B.C.

epsilon appears as early as the fourth century on a roughly-cut *horos* inscription from Attica,[17] and the new forms, as already mentioned, did not oust the old ones even when they were at their most popular.

When all is said and done, the only safe way to undertake, and to have a worth-while opinion about, the dating of a stone on the basis of its lettering is to have a thorough and constantly maintained acquaintance with the comparative material. This is most easily to be obtained by a study of photographs or, better still, of squeezes in a good epigraphic library, and these form the subject of Chapter VII. With this kind of dating experience is essential, and must in particular be based on the site from which the inscription comes and the letter-forms in other texts from the same place or the same area. Judgement regarding the date of an inscription, on the basis of the letter-forms, made 'off the cuff' from a cursory inspection of a squeeze or a photograph of the stone in dispute, is liable to be without much value unless it is made by a scholar already deeply acquainted with all the relevant technicalities. For the average scholar, Attic examples are the easiest of access and perhaps the most usually needed. The development of Attic letter-forms may be conveniently traced by a study of the excellent photographs in J. Kirchner's *Imagines Inscriptionum Atticarum* (ed. 2, 1948), while W. Larfeld, in vol. II of his *Handbuch der Griechischen Epigraphik*, drew up long analytical tables to illustrate the letter-forms used in Attic inscriptions through the centuries: these tables need revision in the light of new material and of new editions of his sources of reference, but they remain for the most part an acceptable guide. It must, however, always be borne in mind that other forms existed contemporaneously with these examples, and that a guide based on Attica is, in the main, good only for Attica. The construction of similar comparative tables for other areas is a task awaiting some future epigraphist, and would be a useful appendix to the epigraphic section of any excavation report. The admirable example of the publication by C. B. Welles of the epigraphy of Gerasa (*Gerasa* (1938), 358–68) could with profit be more widely observed.

Even with all these criteria available to be called into service, it remains in a large number of cases impossible to do more than give an inscription a date within the widest and most general limits. This is particularly the case with many small inscriptions such as tombstones or private dedications from the Levant or Asia Minor or Thrace. It is most important to realise the limitations of these possibilities of dating, especially as historians and students in other classical fields may have to, or would like to, rely upon the epigraphists' opinion about the date of a text, and may be liable to take such an opinion at more than its real worth. It is proper, therefore, to be cautious and hesitant about putting a date to an inscription when the evidence seems barely to allow it. Especially when subjective criteria such as criticism of style are concerned, a robust conservatism cannot be too strongly recommended.

CHAPTER VI

THE RESTORATION OF INSCRIPTIONS

THIS heading probably covers the part of the epigraphist's activity which most generally and readily comes to mind when epigraphy is discussed; it is also the part which provokes the most substantial amount of controversy. The ravages of time and fortune have brought it about that only a minority of inscribed stones which have survived to the present day survive entire and undamaged. They have usually been broken in some degree; perhaps, when a stone has been re-used as a floor or threshold block, its letters have been worn smooth and are barely legible; sometimes one or more of the original edges of the stele remain—although even here appearances may be deceptive, for it may have been trimmed off for re-use as an architectural element in some later building, and its seemingly regular shape may disguise the fact that it is really in a severely mutilated condition. Frequently, however, the only possible description for a surviving inscription is that it is broken on all sides, and 'lapis undique mutilus' recurs time and again in the *lemmata* of published texts. If a stone is broken, and its inscription incomplete for that or other reasons, it is natural to speculate what the remainder of the text said, and how much there was of it. It frequently seems to happen, in a tantalising way, that the surviving piece of an inscription breaks off at the most crucial point, and that it is the missing section which contains the really vital information. There is, of course, the danger of regarding *omne ignotum* as *pro magnifico*, but it is a recurrent experience with all epigraphists that their stone offers just not quite sufficient evidence to set the key to the whole text in their hands. The element of chance is perhaps the most fascinating element in the whole study.

What the editor puts inside his square brackets, and how much he puts there, are up to a point his affair; but they are not necessarily products of his imagination. Some restorations may be thought of as more securely based than others. Unfortunately no device at present exists whereby he can make a distinction between degrees of security, and if he writes 'restorations *exempli gratia*' against his text the *caveat* may easily be, and often is, rapidly overlooked. It is in any case to be doubted whether restorations of this kind are worth including at all.[1] How far he ought, and is entitled, to launch himself into the treacherous currents of epigraphic restoration we shall consider a little later on. First of all it is necessary to look at those features to which he must pay careful regard before he embarks on the hazards of such a voyage. Some of these, such as the date, the historical context, the prosopographical connexions, and the evidence of the archaeology, have been discussed in a previous chapter and need no more than a mention at this point. The editor will presumably not attempt to make restorations out of context as regards material or language.[2] But there are others which must be taken into equally serious account.

Architectural epigraphy. This term is borrowed from B. D. Meritt's *Epigraphica Attica*, a short but fundamentally important study of this aspect of epigraphy which no one even casually interested in the subject can afford to neglect; for anyone making substantial use of epigraphy it should rank as prescribed reading. Its main message is, briefly stated, that we must at all times remember that the stones are architectural monuments with three dimensions, with severe limitations, in consequence of that, as to their size and character. This, like all good maxims, may appear to state an obvious truth; but it is a truth that needs both statement and restatement, since it has been so often overlooked. It is essential, at the very outset, to view the inscription as a piece of architecture and to study it as such. A thin slab, for example, cannot be presumed to have been too wide, or it would have been too thin for the stone-cutter to work on without breaking it; the preserved thickness of the stone must therefore play an integral part in any proposed reconstruction. Or, to take another instance, a broken stele which preserves part of a pediment at the top may yield, from accurate measurement of the latter, a reasonably precise estimate of the inscription's original width, even though the contents of the text itself have proved unhelpful in this direction. Nor must restorations go beyond what the stone might reasonably have contained. Lines cannot be restored *ad libitum* to include what one would like them to have included. They must restrict themselves to the same ration of letters, within limits, as is postulated for their fellows, and they must also restrict themselves to the dimensions, or presumed dimensions, of the stele or monument on which they are inscribed.

It sometimes happens that a newly found fragment proves to be a part of an incomplete inscription already known and published. Attributions or possible attributions of this kind should always be explored as fully as possible before a new piece can be treated as completely isolated and unrelated. This calls for a good knowledge of the relevant material on the part of the epigraphist concerned. Research in a squeeze library will help a great deal; he can check by this means on the content of the inscription and the appearance and size of the letters. But squeezes are not three-dimensional in the epigraphic sense, since they reproduce only the surface of the stone. If, therefore, it is suspected that a new fragment may actually make a join with an old one, the fact must always be tested with the stones themselves. The configuration of the broken stones below the inscribed surface may disprove what looks, from the squeezes, to be a likely join.[3] Or, conversely, the stones may have been broken in such a way that they make a join below the inscribed surface, whereas a study of the surface alone and the evidence of the squeezes would have suggested that no such join was possible.

In making such comparisons of fragments the fate of the stones over the years also has to be taken into account. For example, it may look as if two fragments belong to the same monument, with their lettering and subject-matter apparently in agreement, until it is observed that they have not the same measurement of thickness, even though, in either case, the preserved thickness seems to be original. But it may well have happened that a later re-use of one of the pieces has caused its back to be trimmed down to a thickness less than that of its companion, but with a 'regular' appearance which made it look as if the new back was original and authentic.

Here too the character of the stone must be watched. Paper squeezes and photographs may suggest a common origin for two fragments when in fact one fragment is of marble and the other of limestone. The difference between marbles may also be decisive. There has been much detailed work done recently in this connexion,[4] and some of the criteria which may be invoked are perhaps more exact than the run-of-the-mill epigraphist will have the technical knowledge or the opportunity to use: but in a general way the colour, the grain, and the imperfections of a marble stele may prove instrumental in associating or dissociating fragments attributable or attributed to the same inscription.[5]

It is also possible, by taking the physical properties and appearance of a monument into account, to determine the relative positions of fragments of the same inscription even if they make no physical join at all. In the first place, a study of the contents may suggest that one piece belongs, for example, rather nearer the beginning of the document than another: to this the way in which the material seems to be developing, as compared with other inscriptions of the same type,[6] the presence or absence of formulas known to be generally found towards the beginning or end, and other such considerations all contribute. Or it may be that the language or the formulas on one fragment seem to be continued, though not immediately continued, on another. This may make it possible for the two to be alined vis-à-vis each other and for the lacuna between them to be accurately worked out. But apart from this the matter may be determined by purely physical considerations. Stelae were frequently destroyed by being struck a blow which knocked them over, and from this initial point of impact lines of fracture may radiate in all directions much as they do on a pane of glass hit at one point by a stone. By noting the course and continuation of such lines of fracture, which may also coincide with flaws in the stone itself, fragments perhaps widely separated may be given their relative positions with some degree of accuracy. A notable example of this is the stele (IG I^2 22) illustrated in Plate 1, in which such alinement can be made. It is particularly remarkable for the long curving line of fracture which assures the position of fragment b, at the upper right of the stele, in its correct relationship to the group of contiguous fragments lower down. Fragment b's position in relation to fragment a may be independently determined by the necessary restoration of the opening preamble, parts of which are contained in each, in accordance with the regular formulas.[7]

In the case of a stele destroyed in this way, the damage done would be most serious at the actual point of impact of the blow which demolished it, and any surviving fragments from this area would be likely to be small. This is probably the point (to us) of the most irretrievable loss: farther away from it, fragments would be larger, and more likely, through re-use or otherwise, to have survived. When small fragments do survive to us, it is not unlikely, in consequence, that they will belong, in a group, to the same section of the inscription.[8] But the fate of a stone through the ages may itself produce more small fragments. Even after their discovery and safe keeping in museums or collections, let alone during the many centuries while they remained unnoticed and uncared for, stones have been knocked about and their edges broken.[9] It happens not infrequently that the new editor of a document long since known will make the observation that some letters on the edges, seen by an earlier scholar, have now disappeared. A study of the notes and records of earlier travellers and epigraphic scholars sometimes yields valuable information about stones now mutilated or lost which they were able to see and transcribe before it was too late. This makes it reasonable, in placing a small fragment of an inscription, to look for a close connexion between it and a large piece from which it may have been knocked or chipped at some stage later than the destruction of the monument as it originally stood, and perhaps comparatively recently.

A study of the backs of the stones will often help in this problem,[10] when work on the front yields no profitable result. If the stele is actually opisthographic (i.e. with lettering on the reverse as well as the obverse face), or if it is a rectangular monument of some depth, inscribed on all four sides, the task of fitting the pieces together may present at once greater opportunities and more formidable difficulties. The reconstruction, in the Epigraphical Museum at Athens, of the two great stelae bearing the records of the sixtieth of the allied tribute, paid by the Athenians to the treasury of the goddess Athena, stands as one of the finest examples of this kind of epigraphic skill, and the discussion recorded in vol. I of *The Athenian Tribute Lists*, which explains the location of each piece and the reasons for regarding that location as established, offers an illustration of method which students of epigraphy will digest to their profit.

Stoichedon assistance. The value of the *stoichedon* style as a guide to the restoration of inscriptions has already been mentioned.[11] Once the number of letter-spaces in one line of a *stoichedon* inscription has been established, the number of spaces in all the lines is known, and the possibilities regarding restorations are circumscribed within exact or (taking syllabic division into account) almost exact limits. The establishment of the length of line may itself depend on a consideration which we shall come to next, the recognition of well-known recurrent formulas; but the limits imposed by the requirements of the style serve also to limit possibilities of restoration even in parts of an inscription where these formulas are not in evidence, and many plausible restorations have foundered through disregard of the *stoichedon* pattern. Even when an inscription is not *stoichedon*, the accurate measurement of the average number of letters per line, or in a regular space such as 10 cm., will serve as a useful guide and impose limits which may be slightly more flexible but which will provide a good working basis for restoration. The frequency of the narrow letter *iota* is the chief imponderable factor which has to be taken into account and which allows some latitude here; it is sometimes counted, when an editor shows what he considers to be the number of missing letters, as equivalent to half an ordinary letter: a lacuna reckoned as 2½ letters is likely to be filled by three letters, one of which is an *iota*.

Formulas. Both public and private documents tended to make use of forms of words or phraseology which were fairly well set and stereotyped. The recognition of these on a fragmentary inscription often makes it possible to suggest restorations of the text with some degree of plausibility.[12] It does not take much epigraphic skill to suggest a restoration in, for instance, a fragment of a dedication which reads Μνησικλῆς τῆι Ἥρηι - - - -, where [ἀνέθηκεν] has more than a fifty-fifty chance of being correct. But recurrent formulas, often of considerable length, make the filling of sometimes very substantial lacunas a practicable possibility, according to the type of document concerned. Good examples of this appear among the prytany lists edited by Sterling Dow (*Hesperia* Suppl. I, 1937), in particular no. 79. Here a knowledge of the phraseology customarily used in this type of document, and its variation according to the period of the inscription, enabled the editor to restore very large sections of text even where only a meagre fragment of the stone actually survived, and the restoration, substantial as it was, could be regarded as relatively secure. Where proper names are concerned, an element of doubt is always left. Attic names contain, on an average, eight or nine letters, but it cannot be ruled out that some short name, such as Λέων, might have been present to upset an ingenious restoration based on this average. As a random example of what cannot be restored, *SEG* XII 242 provides an instance of well-known formulas used to fill a lacuna of some thirty letters in the middle of a manumission document: but here the name of the month, and the price of the manumission, must remain unknown and unrestored. The names of the first two councillors given in line 1 come from other evidence relating to the same archonship; the name of the manumitter's son in line 2 is supplied from the patronymic earlier in the line, it being the frequent practice that grandson and grandfather bore the same name (a conjecture further supported in this particular case by the survival of the last two letters of the missing name). In the rest of the text, the restorations are based entirely on the language regularly employed in Delphian documents of this kind.[13]

Preambles are of course particularly valuable, and the formulas regularly used in them frequently provide a good starting-point for analysis of the complete document. In the *stoichedon* text *IG* I² 149 (*SEG* X 105, XII 29), only three or four letters per line survive on a narrow vertical sliver of marble from the centre of the inscription. In line 1 all that remains is EIK: but this is sufficient, with ANEY in the next line, to suggest that the stele was some twenty-five letters wide—a measurement confirmed by the appearance of other formulas lower down in the text—and the restoration of the first two lines can, as a result, be made with reasonable certainty:

[Ἔδοχσεν τ̃ει βολ]ε̃ι κ[αὶ τõι δέμο]-
[ι·...εἰς ἐπρυτ]άνευ[ε, κτλ.]

This whole text, as it appears in *SEG*, is built up on the use of formulas in this way, and is reprinted in full below[14] as an example of what can be done in this direction. But, despite the tolerable accuracy which the use of formulas gives, it must always be admitted that, the greater the quantity of restoration, the greater the margin of error. Even the most apparently secure formula may sometimes betray the trust placed in it.

Occasionally a new fragment may be discovered which makes a join with an already known and edited text, and the acquisition of a new piece of the text itself provides a keen test for the quality and accuracy of any restorations for the section which may have been proposed before it came to light. Even the most plausible and accurate-seeming of skilled restorations may be, and not infrequently are, disproved by these means. On the other hand, it has happened that such new finds have corrected a proposed restoration only in minor details, and the epigraphist's general accuracy and sometimes his exactitude in more minute points may be triumphantly vindicated. Of this a Delphian decree in honour of a doctor Asclepiodorus (*SEG* XIII 361) is a useful instance. The stele on which the honours were recorded was split down the middle. The right-hand piece was discovered, and was edited by L. Robert in 1928; this publication contained ample restoration on the basis of the formulas generally employed in honorary decrees of this type and period.[15] The other half was found and identified more than twenty years later; it joined the old fragment in such a way that only a few small lacunas remained (in the centre towards the top of the inscription), small pieces of the stone having broken away irretrievably at the point of fracture of the two major fragments. The document as reconstituted showed that Robert had not only been generally correct in the restorations he had originally made, but that he had in the majority of instances supplied the very words now shown to have stood on the stone itself.

Not all epigraphists have been so fortunate when new discoveries have subjected the exactness of their work to the most acid of tests; but reliance on formulas as a basis for restoration, assuming that they are properly and intelligently handled, reduces the margin of error considerably, and also reduces the imponderable elements to details of a minor character.

Ethics and security of restoration. In *Epigraphica Attica* (p. 109) B. D. Meritt wrote: 'There will probably always be a division of opinion as to the extent of restoration which is desirable in a fragmentary document. Some restoration can be made with absolute certainty, but for one reason or another the possibility of a sure restoration may become more and more doubtful until finally any restoration suggested would have to be considered in the realm of pure conjecture.' The temptation to restore is strong. The epigraphist may feel that restoration is expected of him. Or, having worked long hours on his text, he may be loth to admit defeat, to say that, after all that study, he just does not know what might have stood on the missing parts of the stone. He may also fear to give occasion for triumph to his colleagues or rivals, who may be prepared to step in where he has refrained from treading. It has already been mentioned that no device is in general use for showing gradations of restoration: the careful inclusion of some such phrase as *exempli gratia* is rapidly overlooked, and a plausible but purely hypothetical restoration may become hallowed by time and used by the non-specialist as evidence to a degree far beyond what the text allows or the editor himself would have wished or permitted.

This being so, it may be better to restrict restorations only to what is reasonably certain on the basis of formulas and similar evidence which is less open to the subjective and hypothetical interpretation of the epigraphist; such a view has been propounded in particular by L. Robert. But 'what is reasonably certain' to one scholar may be the grossest conjecture to another; or a wise restraint may be misunderstood by the more thoroughgoing as mere timidity. It is true that the more one departs from the safe grounds described earlier, the more hypothetical and the more open to criticism a restoration becomes. This is especially so in the case of metrical inscriptions, where whole verses have sometimes been invented by zealous epigraphists, save for a handful of letters still surviving on the stone—a tribute to the scholar's knowledge of his subject but adventurous in the strict sense of epigraphic method. Here again, what is originally meant, and perhaps expressly described, as an attempt to 'give the general sense of a poem' may end by being regarded as the poem itself.

On the other hand, it is asking much of a scholar not to set down the fruits of his labours, especially when few if any know better than he how the lacuna might have been filled; and it is fair to his readers to let them have the benefit of his wisdom. Although epigraphic publications are rich in restorations that should never have been made a part of the definitive text of the inscription, the suggestions ought to have been placed on record somewhere. Perhaps the best solution is to publish a conservative text, which will include restorations regarded as certain or fairly certain not only by the editor himself (who is not, perhaps, an impartial judge) but also by a consensus of his friends. His other suggestions could be made in the *apparatus criticus*, where their segregation would give ample warning that they are to be regarded as more hypothetical and adventurous. Such mutual consultation among scholars is much to be desired of itself; in academic circles considerations of pride and a desire to keep a good thing to oneself too frequently intervene. But certainly as far as the texts are concerned, destined as they are for the use of a wide non-specialist public, self-restraint allied with the maximum of explanation and guidance is the best path to follow. A liberal commentary not only makes clear what is in the editor's mind, but it is of the greatest help to other scholars who, as he may be apt to forget, are not so well acquainted with the intricacies he is talking about as he is himself. It is unfair to those who will use a publication to edit with a rigid austerity *in usum editorum*, and to write in a complacent spirit of academic snobbery only for the happy few. ' Conservatism within limits' will serve as good advice both to beginner and to expert: '*jeux d'esprit*' are not, however, to be disapproved of— rather the reverse, in fact, for they may on occasion turn out to be brilliantly right; but they ought to be clearly marked as tentative, even if the editor secretly feels they deserve a more certain rating than that, and they should be kept in their proper place.[16]

Care and accuracy. These factors should hardly need mentioning, but it is surprising how many errors have been committed in epigraphic study by failure to show care in transcription, failure to make accurate measurements of lacunas, or failure to observe the disposition of words on the stone in cases (especially of gravestones and statue-bases) where the inscription is artistically arranged with a view to balance and decorative effect. It is wise, whenever doubt exists, to draw full-scale facsimiles and work from them; especially is this so where a large stone or substantial lacunas are concerned, and where arrangement or alinement over a considerable area must be worked out. In fact, in these cases it becomes imperative to plot all the measurements and relationships with the strictest care: inscriptions composed of several fragments, all of which have to be exactly related to each other, require a maximum of the most careful drawing and redrawing before it is safe even to begin on any significant amount of restoration either of the monument itself or of the text. 'Facsimile drawings', which often appear in epigraphic publications, are sometimes no more than freehand sketches made in the field, perhaps under conditions of great difficulty, and these are not to be confused with the detailed work of the study. In the case of these field drawings, accuracy depends, of course, on the skill and reliability of the recorder, and in the past such reliance has at times been misplaced. The reliability of the descriptions of stones made by early travellers and epigraphists in Greece sometimes presents serious and even crucial problems. Such drawings should at the least always show the correct letter-forms and reproduce exactly the readings made on the spot, without the intrusion of the recorder's own interpretations or hypotheses; there will be time for them later. The accurate measurements of the monument and of the letters should also be noted on the record in as great a detail as time allows, together with a careful account of the location of the discovery. Errors in recording might well hamper further study of the text, and perhaps of some important subject with which it was concerned, for a long period, until some other epigraphist had time and opportunity to travel out to the locality and re-do what ought to have been properly done in the first place. The student can easily train himself for such work by copying, in the field, stones already known, which he can subsequently check from the publications. It is a labour and discipline, perhaps irksome at the time, which will pay dividends in the long run.

CHAPTER VII

SQUEEZES AND PHOTOGRAPHS

WHILE it is true that many of the stones with which the epigraphist has to deal are small and can easily be carried, and that at times this ease of transport has caused them to move mysteriously from their original location, there are equally many, and perhaps more, which can be moved only with difficulty or which cannot be moved at all. Of these, some must remain as part of the ancient or modern architectural feature which they have long adorned or within which they have been immured; others have been removed to museums where now little short of a major engineering undertaking will alter their position. Smaller stones in museums can often be moved for special purposes of study or photography, but extra labour may be needed and the epigraphist may have the opportunity to exercise his muscle before he can find that of exercising his mind. This, together with the fact that travel to the eastern Mediterranean comes seldom to most classical scholars, means that comparatively few people are able to consider the inscriptions with reference to the actual stones themselves; and even those few may not be in the position to go and look at the stones to verify some particular point when they most want to do so. What is more, those inscriptions which have been found, and still remain, in particularly inaccessible places may rest on the testimony only of one or two scholars who happen to have passed that way in the course of their travels. This puts the epigraphic scholar back at home in his study, as well as the non-specialist, at a disadvantage if he wishes to give some independent thought to a text, and it is at this point that the provision of squeezes, drawings and photographs gives substantial assistance.

The subject of drawings has already been discussed in the previous chapter, and there is nothing more that may be profitably added at this point. Much depends on the observer's accuracy in reading the inscription, and, of the three methods of making a record available to everyone of the stone as it is and looks, that of the line drawing is objectively the least satisfactory.[1] Indeed its chief merit often lies in the very fact that it *is* subjective, and that the eye-witness is recording not so much what is there as what he thought he saw there: but even this merit is best brought out when a squeeze or a photograph is available for purposes of comparison. If the traveller has not squeeze paper, or has run out of film, or has a subject which it is impossible either to photograph or to squeeze, the drawing must perforce suffice; but other methods are to be preferred if they can possibly be carried out.

Squeezes. This is one of epigraphy's less choice technical terms: the irreverent have been known to affect a misunderstanding or misinterpretation of it, and some better noun ought long ago to have been adopted. Official reports often refer, for the sake of clarity, to 'epigraphic squeezes'. In French they are *estampages*, in German *Abklatsche*, in (modern) Greek ἔκτυπα. They are in fact, under whatever name, impressions, usually in paper, of the inscribed surface of a stone, and they preserve what is there to be read in a form convenient for handling, transporting and filing away. It requires a fair amount of practice to be able to make a good squeeze, and it is essential not only to have the opportunity for this but also to have the use of good-quality paper and a brush of a kind specially adapted for the purpose.

The brush should be stout and fairly weighty, should have a handle well adapted to a firm grasp, and should be in general shape rather like a lady's hairbrush, although with a head more rectangular than such brushes are apt to have. It should be some nine or ten inches long (including the handle), and the head should be about four inches wide. The bristles should be set closely together and be fairly soft and supple, as in the brushes used for stippling work by house decorators. The aim of this is that the maker of the squeeze should be able to get a good grasp and even purchase as he beats the paper on to the stone, while at the same time the bristles should be flexible enough not to dig through the paper, tear up its surface, or otherwise do damage to the squeeze while it is being made. The paper most in use is a type of filter paper obtained from laboratory suppliers. It may vary in thickness: a thinner paper needs less working on to the stone, but may disintegrate more easily; a thicker paper is more durable but may take a less fine and precise impression.[2] It may be practicable to use two thicknesses of thinner paper, either retaining the double thickness in the finished squeeze or peeling off the upper layer while the squeeze is still wet: in this latter case less care need be taken, while using the brush, of safeguarding the upper surface of the squeeze. Where no squeeze paper is available, emergency use can sometimes be made of substitutes. Blotting paper disintegrates too readily to be of much value, but if some stiffening agent such as the white of egg is applied to it it will hold together long enough to be useful for subsequent study, provided that it is handled carefully. The stone to be squeezed must first of all be cleaned thoroughly:

otherwise the dirt will transfer itself to the squeeze, which will be grubby and discoloured in consequence. The epigraphist decides how much paper will be needed to cover the area of which he wants the record, and will cut the paper so that it overlaps that area by a fair margin without, however, coming into contact with the ground or anything else from which it could absorb dirt. Once the stone is cleaned and the dirty water wiped off, it should then be wetted again and the paper laid on it; the paper should itself already be moist or should be further moistened when in place on the stone if the moisture it absorbs from the wet stone proves to be insufficient. Then with firm strokes the paper must be beaten against the stone; the effective blows and pressure should come directly at an angle of ninety degrees; glancing blows may move the paper and so blur and spoil the squeeze. It is advisable to begin in the centre of the stone, and to work gradually to the outer edges; places at which the lettering is obscure or fragmentary should receive particular attention, to ensure that every trace will come out on the finished squeeze. If the paper slips, or if it seems that the squeeze will for any other reason not give a sharp and clear impression, it is better to scrap it and begin again. It is never worth attempting to salvage a squeeze once spoiled. When the whole inscribed area has been covered, and the paper worked into every indentation of the surface, with care taken to eliminate air bubbles and pockets which may have been trapped when the paper was brought into contact with the stone, the squeeze can be left to dry. When thoroughly dry it will retain permanently the impression of the surface with which it was in contact, and so offers a valuable means of preserving the record of the stone itself for future use.[3] If possible, squeezes should not be folded, for letters at the point of fold may suffer damage, but for purposes of storage this is sometimes unavoidable. When being transported they should either be kept flat or rolled up loosely. It is most convenient to store them in large cardboard boxes of a measurement of approximately 18 × 24 inches. This accommodates most of the smaller stones, and only a single fold is needed to include a large proportion of the remainder. For very large stones special arrangements need to be made. It is worth noting that, when squeezing a large stone, larger than the size of the sheet of paper which is on hand, more than one sheet may be used, setting the two (or more) side by side with a slight overlap: during the making of the squeeze particular attention should be given to this point of overlap. When dry, if the sheets have been well worked together at their edges, the whole squeeze should come off in one piece. When such joins appear weak, or where tears have been made in the process of taking the squeeze (which is especially liable to happen if there are deep letters, sharp fissures, or abrupt edges to the stone), repairs which do not interfere with the reading of the squeeze are most readily made with transparent tape (such as Scotch Tape). This may need renewal after a few years in storage, and stored squeezes should be regularly inspected for deterioration or other damage.[4]

In the early 1950's experiments in the use of liquid rubber, or latex, for the purpose of making squeezes were carried out by W. K. Pritchett of the University of California, and were followed up at Cambridge with no less success.[5] This liquid rubber is to be had in varying consistencies: that described by Pritchett requires some dilution to make it readily workable, but other types can be poured straight from the bottle. It is advisable to try it out in individual cases, and evolve a personal technique with what one has, before going seriously to work with it in the field. The stone should first be cleaned, either with water and left to dry, or with a thin preliminary layer of rubber which may be peeled off quickly and which should bring the dirt off with it. Then the rubber, in a suitable container and diluted as required, may be spread quickly over the whole surface of the area to be squeezed in a thin layer: the dilution must be fairly accurately assessed, for if the rubber is made too liquid it will not cohere. This thin layer must then be left to dry thoroughly, a process requiring roughly twenty-four hours, after which a second layer can be applied in the same way. Again the dilution of the liquid rubber should be gauged according to the thickness of the squeeze that is needed. Since these squeezes are most useful as translucent records, showing with the light behind them even the most casual mark on the stone, the thin squeeze is often that which the epigraphist will require. With thicker squeezes it is more difficult to obtain an even spread of the rubber, which begins to congeal as soon as it is applied, and it needs some speed and skill to avoid a lumpy surface. Otherwise, it is one of the principal advantages of the use of liquid rubber that it calls for no skill whatsoever, and for no cumbersome paraphernalia of paper, brushes, and cans of water. It may be applied most easily with the back of the hand or with the fingers, and flows of itself into the indentations of the stone without having to be worked in forcibly by the epigraphist, who thus needs to take with him no more than his latex jar and a brush for a preliminary cleaning of the stone. One further item to be recommended for his kit is a jar of corn-starch or a box of French chalk. One of the most difficult processes in squeezing with liquid rubber is that of removing the squeeze from the stone: it needs to be worked off little by little, and there is always the danger that it will

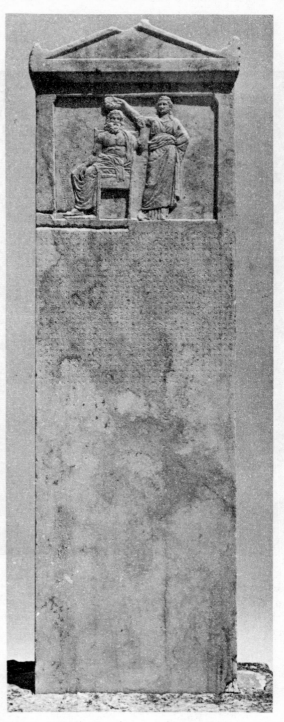

PLATE 3. An Athenian decree making provisions against a
coup d'état, 337 B.C.

PLATE 4. Report of the proceedings of hearings by Roman procurators relating to the upkeep of roads in Phrygia, early third century A.D. Photograph of squeeze. Reproduced by kind permission of the Society for the Promotion of Roman Studies from the *Journal of Roman Studies*, vol. XLVI (1956).

fold back on itself. A dusting of the upper surface with chalk or corn-starch before the process of removal is begun, and an application to the underside as it comes away, will help to prevent this, and will mean also that the squeezes can be stored together without sticking to one another. In storage it is an additional advantage to interleave them with tissue paper. The chalk has also been found to bring into clearer relief some of the less legible letters.

However, liquid rubber for squeezes has certain disadvantages. It cannot, for example, be used on a friable surface. It is also a method which requires that the surface to be squeezed lie flat, and it is less easy to take a squeeze of a large surface all at once.[6] Furthermore it takes time, and is better suited to the requirements of unhurried museum work than to casual squeeze-taking in the field, where time may be of the essence. Its accuracy and precision is probably best fitted to the recording of small controversial areas of an inscription, where every mark counts, and since it picks up the indentations on a nearly smooth surface far more effectively than a paper squeeze it is invaluable for stones on which the lettering has been so worn as to be practically illegible.

With time these squeezes tend to become hard and brittle, and to darken in colour, but they recover their suppleness by being warmed in the hands or moistened under a flow of warm water. Unless they are exceptionally thin, they stand up to handling better than do paper squeezes and recover their shape after being screwed up. It seems un-likely that they will replace the paper squeeze to any great extent, but they should be considered a valuable and at times necessary adjunct to the conventional type.

Since it is the underside of the squeeze, directly in contact with the stone, which receives and retains the direct imprint of the inscription, it is from the underside that a squeeze is most easily and accurately to be read. The upper side has in any case often been roughened and spoiled in the making of the squeeze, but provided that the impression under-neath is good and clear it really matters comparatively little what happens to the upper surface. However, it is worth mentioning that squeezes held up to a light and read from the upper side often yield information not otherwise to be deciphered, so that the upper surface ought not, in the course of making the squeeze, to be deliberately dis-regarded. Translucent liquid rubber squeezes, as noted above, are also best read this way. But in the ordinary course of events squeezes are as it were read backwards: a good strong light and a magnifying glass are essential parts of the epigraphist's equipment in dealing with them, and since they can be picked up and turned from this angle to that, for the light to strike them at different points and from different directions, they frequently can be made to provide more detail than could have been won from a study of the stone itself, and they are often, for the same reason, a good deal easier to read. Accurate and careful reading of squeezes is, again, something which all students of epigraphy ought to practise regularly, progressing from those that are clear and straightforward to those that are practically illegible. At the same time, one must sound the warning that it is easy, both on the squeeze and on the stone, to read too much. After a long spell of study of the problems of a particular inscription it becomes dangerously possible to convince oneself of being able to see what indeed one wants to see, and to mistake for letters on the squeeze marks which in fact reproduce some flaw or other mark on the surface of the stone without significance for the inscription.

Most scholars with even a casual interest in epigraphy who have travelled in Greece and been able to secure some paper have brought back squeezes for the purposes of their own work. But in one or two places where epigraphy is an especial subject of study, the collection of squeezes has been carried on on a systematic basis, in an attempt to create a library of inscriptions. It is even true to say that in these centres inscriptions can be compared and studied in a way impossible in the Aegean area itself, where the relevant stones may be physically far apart from each other. A squeeze library makes comparative study feasible and effective, and provides, readily available for consultation, an epigraphic record which supplements and checks that offered by the printed texts as set out in the *corpora* (for which see Chapter IX). The oldest and largest of these collections is that of the Deutsche Akademie der Wissenschaften in Berlin, which fortunately survived the perils of the Second World War. That at the Institute for Advanced Study in Princeton, New Jersey, is especially strong in Attic inscriptions, and further contains the complete record of the inscriptions discovered in the course of the fruitful excavations of the American School of Classical Studies in the Athenian Agora. The collection of the Museum of Classical Archaeology at Cambridge, the most recently established, also has its main strength in its collection of Attic inscriptions, but it has a growing collection of material from other parts of the Greek world, most notably from Asia Minor. There is, in addition, a useful squeeze collection at the Ashmolean Museum in Oxford, to which accessions are made from time to time. Scholars at all these centres are always willing to answer queries which may be resolved by a study of the squeezes in their possession and to make available in whatever way they can the benefits of having at hand, in one place, the exact facsimiles of thousands of stones which could have been brought together in no other way.

But a small personal squeeze collection is within reach of any classical scholar interested in the subject: it is a possibility, furthermore, which seems to have been overlooked by schools, where the importance of inscriptions in the teaching of ancient history is perhaps less appreciated than it might be; here squeezes would provide the most useful illustrative material. A personal record of the *ipsissima verba* of the great kings or the sovereign assemblies brings us into a direct and immediate relationship with the ancient world which we study, and a good squeeze of a significant inscription provides for all who care to use it a stimulating witness to reinforce and enliven the pages of the literary texts; for these, even if they be the accounts of contemporaries, sometimes seem from their long history of transmission to have a remoteness which the direct evidence of the epigraphy, speaking without intermission straight from the ancient world to the modern, recording the action as and when it took place, notably lacks.

Photography. These same sentiments apply no less to photographs than to squeezes of inscriptions, although photographs can provide only a record of the appearance of the stone and are less valuable than the direct impression of the squeeze. Nevertheless, photographs frequently bring out some features or aspects of an inscription which even a good squeeze fails to illustrate, especially as regards the colour and below-surface appearance of the stone; they preserve, for filing and library purposes, the picture of the stone as it looks in a way that the squeeze cannot, and for the most part reveal the physical characteristics of it which, as has already been remarked, are vital to the proper study of an inscription.[7] While providing no substitute for a good squeeze, they must be regarded as a necessary complement to it, and an epigraphist in editing a text should ideally be in possession of both photographs and squeeze while he is at work.

For an effective photograph it is necessary to have effective lighting. In the field, especially on tour, it may be that little is possible beyond the casual snapshot; not every traveller carries a tripod and a set of special lenses about with him. But a little extra equipment and a little extra care may even in these conditions produce valuable results. Nevertheless, snapshots do not generally make good illustrations to learned articles, and modern methods both in photography and in journal illustration have tended to bring about a great improvement in the quality of published photographs. It may of course happen that a description of a text is best illustrated not by a picture of the stone itself but by a photograph of the squeeze. This may be the case not only where the stone is in such a position that it cannot be photographed at all, while the portable squeeze made from it can be taken away and photographed at leisure: sometimes, on a stone where the lettering has been worn particularly smooth, the traces are not readily visible on a photograph of the actual stone, but show up better on the squeeze. In these cases the squeeze should be photographed from the more legible (i.e. the under) side, and the photograph printed in reverse.

For the purposes of photographing the stone itself, the problem in a museum revolves around the availability of adequate lighting, and special apparatus will usually be necessary. In the open, especially in the conditions of the eastern Mediterranean, this is not ordinarily a problem, except where an inscription is fixed in a shadowed position and cannot be moved.[8] Otherwise the difficulty may be that of too much direct light, rather than too little. What is required in all cases is so to manage the lighting that it falls obliquely on the surface of the inscription, in order to leave one side of the cut of the letters in shadow: a flat, 'straight-on' light is a hindrance rather than a help to legibility, since (unless the letters are filled in with paint) it is the shadow formed by the cutting that makes the lettering of an inscription clear to read. Ideally therefore an inscription requires to be photographed twice, once lighted from the left and once from the right, or, perhaps better, from upper left and upper right, if there is likely to be any dispute about its reading. On the other hand, it may be more desirable to give one photograph only of the *ensemble* and, if equipment for the taking of close-up pictures is available, to concentrate on those areas of the stone which are likely to present the greatest difficulty.

It is not the present purpose to discuss the photographic technicalities in detail; these can best be studied from the manuals of photography and especially from M. B. Cookson's study of the photographic side of archaeological work.[9] In regular excavations, naturally, special arrangements for photography exist and one member of the party with particular photographic training is entrusted with the photographic record of the site and the discoveries made there. Where an epigraphist is working on his own, without the benefit of professional or skilled amateur advisers, he may have to rely on the quality of his camera and his own ingenuity in triumphing over the difficulties and making use of the advantages that the circumstances may provide. But he would be well advised to devote some time to the study and practice of amateur photography before he ventures forth: the record he may make or mar could be uniquely valuable. It is possible, even in these conditions, to produce work of real quality and of subsequent value for later and more leisured work in the study. Small cameras, especially the popular 35 mm. size, make it possible to attempt a number of photographs of a single object without great inconvenience or expense. Colour photography can assist particularly in drawing attention to the discoloration and those imperfections of a stone which, as already noted, may play a substantial part in the proper editing of an inscription; but at present the enlargement of coloured photographs, the making of colour positives from the ordinary colour transparencies, and their reproduction as illustrations in books and magazines present their own problems, not least the problem of expense, and this leaves black-and-white photography still the most suitable for this type of work. It is, however, a growing practice to maintain two cameras, one for each kind of film, in which case a colour picture of the entire stone can be reinforced by a concentration in black-and-white on points of particular difficulty.

These reflections cannot, in any case, serve as more than a general guide to the beginner. He must get to know his own equipment and its possibilities under a variety of conditions: it is ultimately only by a process of trial and error (preferably with well-known stones, where failure is not irretrievable) that he can acquire the technique which will make even a hurried photograph, snatched during the temporary halt of a Turkish bus, a valuable contribution to epigraphic scholarship.

CHAPTER VIII

INSCRIPTIONS IN THE HISTORY OF GREEK ART

THE place of inscriptions in the general setting of Greek artistic development seems, hitherto, to have interested neither the epigraphist nor the art historian. Yet inscribed stelae may be regarded not only in the light of the subject-matter provided by the inscription but as part of the architecture or sculpture of the time; for each inscription is as it were a minor architectural product, and the art of lettering, although a province to itself, is akin to that of sculpture in general and of relief sculpture and decorative architectural ornament in particular. For the most part, however, epigraphists have been concerned with their inscriptions as three-dimensional objects only in so far as, along the lines set down in Chapter VI, this enables them the better to elucidate the problems of the texts. As far as the decorative elements are concerned, attention has concentrated itself upon the reliefs or other sculpture with which the inscription is associated. This last is natural enough where, for example, the inscription consists of an artist's signature or a dedication or title of a statue, or where it is a question of a legend accompanying a grave-relief.[1] Small bas-reliefs which sometimes adorn in a subsidiary way, and serve to illustrate the contents of, an inscription which was, at the time, no doubt regarded as of some importance and worthy of the additional expense, as in Plate 3, have been the subject of separate study.[2] Nevertheless the artistry involved in setting out and inscribing a stele deserves to take its place among the minor arts of the classical world. A well-inscribed text, whether by the austere and unadorned regularity of its simple letters and *stoichedon* pattern, or whether because of the wealth of its decorative elements and the symmetry of its layout, has an aesthetic appeal of its own, and this may and should be studied in much the same way as are other branches of Greek art. The same principles will apply, and the same canons hold good. The quality of epigraphic art can exercise an attraction (or the reverse) for the individual, as is the case with other artistic fields: but eulogies of the beauty of Greek inscriptions in general terms, based as they must be on a subjective appreciation, would be profitless in this context. The reader must look at the inscriptions for himself and form his own judgement. We ought, however, to look more closely at

86

epigraphy as representative of the art of its time: the distribution in the Greek world of epigraphic quality as well as quantity, the artistic composition of an inscription, and the historical development of epigraphy as an art-form should all be considered as necessary to the proper study of the subject.

All of these fields deserve a more detailed treatment than is the present purpose, and this brief mention 'potest videri ostendisse posteris, non tradidisse'. In particular, it would be necessary either to illustrate this book more profusely than its scope permits, or to have at hand a volume of good photographs of assorted inscriptions, widely varied in origin, date and subject, and this is not available. It would be expensive to produce, and would lack the wide market on which picture books on Greek art in general, or photographs of the Greek countryside and antiquities, are able to draw. The nearest approach to such a work is still the *Inscriptiones Graecae* (Bonn, 1913) of Otto Kern, the examples in which are largely Attic, with a few photographs of stones from the islands, Pergamum, Priene and elsewhere. The photographs were very good for their time, but a comparison with J. Kirchner's *Imagines Inscriptionum Atticarum* (ed. 2, 1948) shows what they now lack in interest and vitality. Kirchner's book, as its name indicates, confines itself to Attic material; it is invaluable for showing the development of the letter-forms in Athenian inscriptions (see Chapter v, p. 65), and, thereby, for bringing out the artistic quality both of the lettering style in detail and of the inscriptional composition in general.

For other areas it remains necessary to consult the individual publications relating to each, so that it is impossible, without a large number of such volumes ready to hand, to make any easy comparison of style and development. As was mentioned in the previous chapter, most publications of inscriptions now provide good drawings or photographs, or possibly both; but this none the less means that all the publications must be available where and when they are required. The four volumes of *Inscriptiones Creticae* illustrate every stone of any significance; all the stones published in the course of the excavations in the Agora of Athens have been accompanied by photographs, and these sometimes offer a synopsis of artistic quality in inscriptions. For example, plates 55–60 in *Hesperia* XXIII (1954) show a selection of battered grave inscriptions of periods ranging from the fourth century B.C. to the second century A.D., which are useful for illustration and comparison of lettering. But it is not always possible to illustrate the material adequately; the cost of plates adds enormously to the cost of a book, and *Inscriptiones Creticae* stands alone among publications of that size in the extent of its illustrations. For Asia Minor and the Levant, the only real possibility in any case is to note examples which serve as illustrations for epigraphic studies, as, for instance, those of Jeanne and Louis Robert, or for periodicals such as *Syria* in which epigraphic material is a principal or at least an important topic of discussion.[3] But it seems as a result both advisable and necessary, for ease of reference, to confine any examples used for present purposes to the illustrations of Kern and Kirchner, which are to be found in most classical libraries; although this will involve an undue concentration on Attica it will perhaps serve to underline a survey in general terms of the historical development of epigraphic art, in its relation to the overall artistic development of the Greeks.

Broadly speaking, the fashions and tendencies discernible in Greek epigraphy run fairly closely parallel with those which influenced the history of Greek sculpture. Although the epigraphic masters remain anonymous, epigraphy underwent similar developments to those associated in sculpture with Polycleitus, Pheidias and Lysippus. It had its high archaic style; in the fourth century it acquired something of that languorous polish one might characterise as Praxitelean; in the Hellenistic period it evolved a baroque of the type often, from the style of the Great Altar of Pergamum, referred to as Pergamene, and in its small way mirrored both the graces and the excesses of that artistic phase. Finally, in the Roman period, there is developed a classical eclecticism, akin to that of the Pasitelean school; this is replaced to some degree, under the early Empire, by new decorative forms, which can perhaps be designated as 'Greco-Roman Imperial', and these lead on by a direct transmission into the stiff and stylised epigraphic treatment of the early Byzantine Empire.

(*a*) *The Archaic period.* In Athens this may be said to end about 480 B.C. In other regions it continued longer, in places through the greater part of the fifth century. In this period the epichoric alphabets found some regularity of form, as was described in an earlier chapter, the letters became more regular and more precise in their construction, and a feeling for the form and arrangement of the inscription began to develop. Both vase-painters and architects recognised and appreciated the decorative quality of letters and used them for that purpose (Kirchner 8–9). The Attic 'Little Master' cups make a particularly effective use of inscriptions as a feature of the decoration, and the decorative character is emphasised by the fact that in some cases the 'inscriptions' are meaningless strings of letters added solely as part of the vase's ornamentation. The artists of the archaic gravestones sometimes worked the lettering of the accompanying inscription skilfully into the overall design. The

architect of the Stoa of the Athenians at Delphi gave a special prominence to the inscription, the monumental character of which added to
the concept and the effect of the building as a whole. Letter-forms in
this period, from rough beginnings (Kirchner 4–5), rapidly developed in
quality and in arrangement (Kirchner 10). This was also the period of
the growth of the *stoichedon* style, which has been more fully discussed in
Chapter III; it began tentatively (Kern 7, left) but later reached a high
point of precision and grace (Kirchner 13; Kern 13, top). Nevertheless,
outside Attica the development was less rapid; the Corinthian memorial
of the battle of Salamis, the monument of a great event set up by a great
city, is illustrative of the difference in achievement (Kern 9, bottom).

(*b*) *The Pheidian–Polycleitan period.* The growth of the Athenian
democracy imposed a greater need for the expeditious engraving of
public business. Yet, without any sacrifice of beauty in detail or in
arrangement, the artists contrived to limit their spatial requirements.
The middle and the third quarter of the century showed the Attic
stoichedon style at its best and most vigorous: there is a strength and
virility about the fine work of the time (Kirchner 33–6), and even the
second-class products (Kern 14, bottom) have a strongly architectonic
quality in their composition and an assurance in the handling of the
problems of inscriptional engraving. Where Athens had led, other
parts of Greece began to follow (Kern 5, left; 10, centre), and by the
end of the century had achieved a full competence (Kern 16, left). The
Olympian qualities of the epigraphic art of the Periclean period, and
the completion of the development both of the forms of the individual
letters and of the *stoichedon* style, resulted in an epigraphic impasse
similar to that produced by the Polycleitan canon. Kirchner 41 (Plate 2
above), an often-quoted but always satisfactory example of the best
Attic inscriptional work, looks, like Polycleitus' *Doryphoros*, both backwards and forwards. It sums up the development of the previous
centuries and states its final achievement, and it also sets a problem for
the fourth century to resolve. If things cannot be done better, they must
be done differently. And already, at the same time, a lighter, less robust,
yet more delicate quality begins to make its appearance (Kirchner 40),
just as Polycleitus' own *Diadoumenos* contains much of the character that
was to become distinctively that of the sculpture of the following century.

Among the qualities which particularly distinguish the best work of
the later fifth (and indeed the early fourth) century epigraphic artists is
the regard paid to the overall layout of the inscription and its relationship to the stele on which it is inscribed. The stele was carefully made in
harmonious proportions of height and width, and the introduction of

the tapered stele added a new and pleasing element to it. The text was generally placed at a height convenient for the reader, and the use of lettering of a different size in the heading, especially in the first part of the fourth century, with the resulting contrast not only valuable in making the inscription easier to read and more arresting but also adding variety and liveliness to the entire monument, further showed their concern with the artistic value of their productions. Finally, the adoption of the cornice surmounting the stele added a great deal to the beauty of the monuments and, by serving to protect the lettering from the weather, had a utilitarian purpose also. The total effect is of an artistic harmony which is not merely decorative but which serves practical ends at the same time; the success of the epigraphic artists of this period, reflecting that of their colleagues in other artistic fields, was unequalled either before or since, and deserves greater notice than it has hitherto won.

(c) *The fourth century.* Initially, and especially outside Attica, this repeated the same forms that had characterised the later fifth century (Kern 22, top right); and in Athens itself there is much that, allowing for the official change to the Ionic alphabet in 403 B.C., shows no change from the best that the preceding period produced (e.g. Kirchner 49). But decrees became longer, and the letters therefore smaller. This at times, as mentioned above, made an effective contrast with the use of larger letters for the heading or prescript (Kirchner 43; Kern 19), and was for a time a favourite device. On the other hand, haste and the need for compression led often to rough workmanship and to carelessness in the construction of letters (Kirchner 50; 52). Only the *stoichedon* order kept the composition together, and even this was not always the case (Kirchner 54). Yet, despite these limitations, work was often of a fine quality, which compensated for its loss of the vigour and *bravura* of the fifth century by a new characteristic of grace and charm (Kirchner 59; Kern 27, top). When smaller letters are used they often have what Austin called a 'pusillanimous character' (Kirchner 63), and although they sometimes suit the *stoichedon* style excellently and make a pleasing and regular composition (Kirchner 62) they are ill suited to a wide *stoichedon* spacing (Kern 29, right), and their use helped to break up the style as a useful and aesthetically desirable medium. What happened when it was abandoned was already becoming obvious (Kern 29, left).

(d) *The Hellenistic period.* The fifth-century legacy of the classical style was fast expiring by the end of the fourth century, and it was clear that a thoroughgoing change was in prospect. The shift of political emphasis from Greece to Asia meant that there, and no longer in Attica, was prosperity to be found and the best epigraphic work done. Athens, once the most epigraphically progressive city, becomes conservative, and Attic examples may not be taken as representative of the best of their epoch. A new tendency to decorative effect in lettering, later to flower in the baroque usage of apices, becomes noticeable in the fourth century both in Athens (Kirchner 62) and in Asia (Kern 31, top), where the ends of the letters are enlarged to a wedge shape. An inscription from the same place (Priene) and of roughly the same date shows the new decorative character of non-*stoichedon* writing, with its ribbon-like effect of strips of writing, the letters being closely packed horizontally and leaving by way of contrast a good clear space vertically between the lines (Kern 31, bottom). This can be artistically most effective (Kern 32, top left), especially when the inscription calls for variety in size (Kern 33, top). Meanwhile, the decorative character of the individual letters lent an additional artistic flavour to the inscriptions (Kern 33, bottom), but when this was badly done (Kern 35, top; 39, top right; Kirchner 117) the results were the more notably miserable. It should be noted not only that Athens continued to produce work of varying quality under the old canons (Kirchner 95–103) without adopting the newer and more fanciful decorative forms, but that in general a simpler and more classical style continued to exist alongside the baroque (Kern 39, top left), and this later received a rebirth of vigour in the imperial classicism of the principate.

(*e*) *The Roman period.* By the end of the Hellenistic age the two prevailing 'schools' of epigraphic art, the classical and the baroque, began to draw together and, as it were, to meet one another half way. The new political order in the ancient world produced also an artistic tranquillity which, if lacking the adventurousness born of the stimulus of the uncertainties of earlier times, evolved a quiet and artistically pleasing kind of classicistic synthesis. Aesthetically the best work of the principate and early Empire is the most satisfactory of all, showing excellence of composition and structure in the individual letters combined with judicious application of decoration avoiding some of the excesses of the past (Kern 38, top; 42). Earlier motifs were continued (Kirchner 125), and indeed it may sometimes be impossible to distinguish, on artistic criteria alone, work of the Hadrianic from work of the Hellenistic period (Kern 43, top; cf. p. 63 above). Epigraphy seemed however to have regained a balance it had lost in the fourth and third centuries (Kern 44, bottom), and settled to a long period of steady if uninspired adequacy (Kirchner 143, 144; Plate 4 below). But at the same time the introduction of new letter-forms (above, pp. 64–5) and a growing tendency to carelessness even in official and monumental inscriptions began to interrupt the general placidity which had come to characterise the epigraphic art. On good work the effect of the new forms was sometimes pleasing (Kern 47, top left; Kirchner 145, 146); but in general the results were poor (Kern 48, left), and even the qualities of the surviving classicism began, as time went on, to be lost also (Kirchner 147).

In considering the form and style of Greek inscriptions of the Roman epoch it is essential to bear in mind the relationship between Greek and Latin epigraphy at the time. Very great advances were made during the last century B.C. in the quality, both technical and artistic, of Latin inscriptions, and the half-century between Sulla and Augustus wrought a remarkable transformation in the whole epigraphic achievement of the Romans. It may be suggested that the influence of Greek models was strongly at work during this period, and that Greek masters in the skills of epigraphy were called in to provide an artistic leaven for Rome no less than were the sculptors and painters. On the other hand, once monumental epigraphy was fairly launched in the West, it maintained a character and impressiveness distinctively its own, itself later to provide the models for the Renaissance printers and the lettering styles of the Western world.

The style of Greek inscriptions of the later first, and particularly the second, centuries A.D. makes it seem likely that the Greeks' gift had returned to them with dividends, and that they in their turn had profited by the influence of Rome. The introduction of cursive forms also may have been not unaffected by the parallel development in the West. The supposition of this two-way influence, from Greece to Rome in the late Republic and from Rome to Greece under the principate, goes some way towards explaining the notable and swift epigraphic development of Rome as well as towards accounting for the architectonic character of much Greek work of the age of Trajan and Hadrian, which, beautiful as it is, often seems sterile and mechanical. The Romans saw more clearly than the Greeks the mechanistic side of epigraphy: to them it seemed to belong, artistically speaking, not with sculpture but with architecture. And this regard for the architectural quality of an inscription, and its relationship to its surroundings, seems to have affected Greece also, restoring the balance of form discussed above, but eradicating much of the individuality and liveliness of the work of the previous period.

This short survey has been constructed around the most readily available illustrations, but, with these in mind, the reader may go on to study other material illustrated elsewhere, and will find that, generally speaking, the broad lines of development here laid down remain good. He should, however, pay particular regard to the epigraphy of Asia Minor, where the Hellenistic period has left its best work. It seems true to say that, while fashions changed, the technical qualities and, on the whole, the artistic good taste of the epigraphic craftsmen remained fairly constant. The breakdown of the Attic tradition left them with problems which ultimately found a solution in the reunion of divergent tendencies in the later first century B.C., and in a rejuvenated classicism in the early Empire. But the experiments of the Hellenistic period, even when their applied decoration was at its most fanciful, never lost a firm sense of composition, which makes a good piece of inscriptional work, of whatever period, a thing of beauty.

The quality of the best epigraphic artists unfortunately also serves to bring into relief the poverty of local and provincial work, as exemplified for instance by dedications and grave inscriptions from the interior of Anatolia or from Thrace or Moesia under the Roman Empire. But just as there were crude rustic cult images set up while Praxiteles was creating the Cnidian Aphrodite, so there was rough and poor work at all stages of epigraphic development. We have here concentrated attention on the best that inscriptional remains can offer, in order to suggest its proper relationship to work of high quality in other artistic fields and to set it in the picture of Greek artistic history. Did more inscriptions survive complete and unmutilated, we should be in a better case to make a reasonable assessment of that relationship. But at least we are, throughout, in the presence of original work; we are not compelled, as are for instance students of Greek sculpture, to see the ancient master-pieces mainly at second hand. However, to counterbalance this, we must admit that we do not know the name even of a single epigraphic artist; the 'artists' signatures' which accompany many statue bases were perhaps the work of professional lettering-engravers, and were not written by the sculptors themselves, although in a few cases, especially in the archaic period, artist and inscription-writer may have been one and the same person. Nor can we refer, except in the most general terms, to 'schools' of epigraphy. It has, on one or two occasions, been possible to isolate 'hands', but work in this direction has not progressed far, nor is it likely to do so, since the diversity in detail among the surviving inscriptions is remarkable. The most that can be done is to suggest that the trends which affected the art of epigraphy can be seen to be those which affected Greek art in general, and that the study of inscriptions on this basis is one from which archaeologists, art historians, and epigraphists themselves can alike derive profit.

CHAPTER IX

EPIGRAPHIC PUBLICATIONS

IT was observed in an earlier chapter that there are few scholars who find themselves in a position to consult the stone itself when they wish to quote or to study an inscription, and not many who are able, without some trouble and difficulty, even to consult a squeeze or a photograph of it. Nor, even if they did so, would they be in possession of all the facts about it that they ought to have. They would still not know the details of any restorations which had been suggested for it, or of the comments made on its date or its contents, as elaborated and worked into the existing body of received knowledge of the ancient world by scholars earlier than themselves. It is necessary, as a result, whether one can see the stone (or some facsimile of it) or whether one cannot, to have some ready and easily available means of knowing where a given text is published, and what subsequent work has been done upon it since its initial publication. The number of inscriptions now known, and the amount of work which has been done upon them, are alike so bulky and scattered that it is only by uniting information about them into a uniform series of volumes, and by giving them a reference number so that it is possible to talk about them with the ease of a simple numerical quotation, that the texts can be satisfactorily collected and made available for general use. But even when a text has been incorporated into such a collection, work on its improvement still goes on, and it continues to offer material, directly or indirectly, for learned studies on this or that aspect of classical civilisation: so that on both scores further treatment of it will reappear in a variety of publications, and it becomes again more than possible for a scholar to be in ignorance of some reference he ought to have quoted for work done on an inscription with which he is dealing. Without a freedom from commitments given to few academics, it is impossible adequately to keep abreast of the flood of learned literature which flows so abundantly from the pens of classical scholars. There is thus a twofold problem confronting the man who wishes to make use of the evidence of epigraphy: Where can he find the most important publication of the inscription he is looking for, and how can he find out about any work done on it since that publication was made? The answers can be listed, roughly speaking, under two separate headings, 'The *Corpora*' and

'The Supplementary Publications', and it is as well, therefore, to deal with each of these in turn.

The Corpora. Collections of inscriptions, both in Latin and Greek, published as an *ensemble* have a long history.[1] The earliest attempt since the end of the classical age to transcribe epigraphic monuments is preserved in a manuscript collection of inscriptions copied by a traveller in Italy in the ninth or tenth century A.D., known as the Anonymus Einsiedlensis. This epigraphist, like many who were to follow him, mixed Latin and Greek together (only two of the Anonymus' inscriptions are in fact Greek), and found in the classical remains of Italy a rich source of epigraphic interest. Most prominent in the early history of epigraphy, as far as Greece was concerned, was Cyriacus of Ancona (*ob. c.* 1455), a merchant who copied inscriptions in the course of his commercial journeys in the Aegean, at the farthest extent of which he even penetrated to Egypt and noted down material there. The inscriptions he collected were published and formed the basis of a number of other small *Corpora* of inscriptions in succeeding centuries, his nucleus being added to as new material was discovered and transcribed. The usual method of presentation was that of grouping the inscriptions according to their place of origin, and some publications began to concentrate on specific geographical areas. This system was criticised by the Dutch scholar Martin Smetius (*ob. c.* 1574), who preferred a method based on the type and character of the inscription, rather than to break up material which, by content, belonged together simply because different examples were found in different geographical locations. The two methods are in fact not compatible, but both are needed, and both flourish with equal usefulness at the present time. These early studies are rather of interest in the history of scholarship than of value for modern epigraphic studies, but it does sometimes happen that a stone copied by a Renaissance scholar has disappeared since his time, and that his text has therefore to serve as the sole basis of our knowledge. Unfortunately the accuracy of these early epigraphists cannot be relied on, nor did they invariably note all the features which a modern copyist would look for in recording the details of a stone, so that, in using them as evidence, it is always necessary to consider the general reliability and the idiosyncrasies of the author in question. However, by degrees, and arranged as they were by geographical regions, these publications began to assume the basic form of a *Corpus Inscriptionum* as we understand it.

Apart from the notes of travellers and their progressive publication in a *Corpus* form, individual collectors of antiquities edited and described the stones in their possession as an entity to themselves. A notable example of this kind of publication is that of the Marmora Arundelliana, a collection preponderantly of Greek material amassed by Thomas Howard, Earl of Surrey, published in 1628, and subsequently presented to the University of Oxford, where it formed the basis of further publications over the next one hundred and fifty years. Publications of this kind were the predecessors of the 'Museum-publications', which will be dealt with later; these publish a museum's collection of inscriptions as a unity, complementary to the *Corpus* in which the same inscriptions will be scattered according to their original provenience.

Publications by travellers continued to form the main basis for epigraphic study, and their texts, copied in the field and described and edited in their accounts of their travels or their studies of the region which they had visited, were from time to time incorporated into the definitive publications, where they took their places beside the inscriptions already known from the same region or (on the Smetius principle) inscriptions from elsewhere of the same type. The line of such works is a direct one from Cyriacus, through Jacob Spon and Sherard in the seventeenth and eighteenth centuries, Le Bas,[2] Foucart and Waddington in the nineteenth, to Keil, von Premerstein, Hula and Szanto at the end of the same century and to modern traveller-scholars such as George Bean and Sir William Calder (whose years of study in Asia Minor form the foundation of the most bulky of such 'travel-publications', the *Monumenta Asiae Minoris Antiqua*). These epigraphical journeys are nowadays the result less of a casual search after inscribed stones in out-of-the-way places than of a carefully organised expedition aiming to study some particular historical or topographical problem which the discovery of epigraphic material can often help to solve.

This use of newly discovered inscriptions in the development of a particular field of study, especially of topography, leads us to a further type of epigraphic publication, the 'Theme-publication'. We may include under this head such works as that of Jean Pouilloux on the history and cults of Thasos, in which both new and already known material is co-ordinated and incorporated into a general study amounting to a full-scale history of the island, or that of Bean and P. M. Fraser on the possessions of the Rhodian state on the mainland of south-west Anatolia, in which the newly discovered texts are in fact kept separate, although they form an essential part of the general historical study and are built round a discussion of the identification of the mainland sites over which Rhodian rule extended.[3] 'Theme-publications' of this kind in their turn begin to shade into a third *Corpus*-category—that already mentioned as favoured by Smetius—which collects into a single volume or series of volumes inscriptions relating to the same subject; these may be described as 'Type-collections'. Here, among many examples which might be cited, it is perhaps sufficient to instance such collections (often with an extensive commentary included) as the *Leges Graecorum sacrae e titulis collectae* of J. von Prott and L. Ziehen, *Lois sacrées de l' Asie mineure* of F. Sokolowski, the *Corpus Inscriptionum Iudaicarum* of J. B. Frey, C. B. Welles' *Royal Correspondence in the Hellenistic Period*, and the *Recueil des inscriptions juridiques grecques* by R. Dareste, B. Haussoullier and Th. Reinach. Such collections are not necessarily based on a personal review of the stone on the writers' part, any more than is the case with a definitive *Corpus*-publication itself on the usual geographical lines, although it is desirable that an editor who sets out to form such a documentary source-book should have an opportunity to reconsider the texts of as many stones as possible, since his command of the comparative material on that subject may well be greater than that of the stone's original editor or of the editor of the *Corpus* into which it may have been incorporated since its original publication.

In this group of *Corpus* publications, then, we have set together the collected material of epigraphically-minded travellers or travel-minded epigraphists, published as an *ensemble* either (*a*) in their own travel-accounts or (*b*) in extended studies or 'theme-publications' relating to the area in which they have an especial interest, and (*c*) collections of material, usually from already-published sources, uniting inscriptions of a single type. It remains to discuss the principal type of publication in this group, so far mentioned only *en passant* as having evolved from the early travel-collections, the *Corpus Inscriptionum Graecarum* itself. Until the beginning of the nineteenth century, collections of inscriptions from the Renaissance onwards had included Greek and Latin material together. It was August Boeckh who, under the auspices of the Prussian *Akademie der Wissenschaften* at Berlin, undertook the publication of a new and comprehensive *Corpus*, designed to reunite all Greek inscriptional material already published and to present it in a uniform and accessible manner. The first section of this work, later completed in four folio volumes, appeared in 1825, but even while it was in the process of publication the growing amount of epigraphical exploration by scholars of various nations, such as Le Bas, Newton, Pittakys, K. Keil and others, as well as a rising interest in general epigraphical problems, instanced for example by the publication in 1840 of Franz's fundamental *Elementa Epigraphices Graecae*, began to make it out of date. The indices to the whole of Boeckh's *Corpus* were finally

published in 1877, by which time the discovery of new texts and the discussion of the old had brought the Berlin Academy to a decision to
undertake *ab initio* a new version of the *Corpus*. The old *CIG* remains
the only modern *Corpus* to embrace the whole of the Greek world. Its
successor, which remains incomplete, was after some changes of title
finally designated *Inscriptiones Graecae* (*IG*). A guide to the original
titles of the early *IG* volumes, sometimes quoted as references in books
of the time and therefore useful to have at hand, is given in the appendix
to this chapter, in which are listed the volumes of *Inscriptiones Graecae*
so far published and the areas with which they are concerned. *IG*, like
CIG, was planned on the geographical system; its first volumes dealt
with Attica, and those which followed covered the remainder of Greece,
Italy, and the western provinces of the Roman Empire. But not all the
volumes projected have been completed. Gaps remain, some of them so
adequately filled by other publications that there is now no need in these
areas to complete the original plans. Despite the difficulties of modern
conditions, and the interruptions caused by World War II, work on the
great undertaking continues, in particular with *IG* vol. x (Macedonia)
and some parts of xII, which covers the Aegean islands with the exceptions of Delos and Crete.

Yet, even while *IG* was being compiled, it became necessary to begin
the revision of those parts of it already published, and the new edition is
now known as the *editio altera*, distinguished from its predecessor by the
use of a small figure 2 in the citation (*IG*²). So far, this second edition
has extended only to Attica (*IG* I² and II²), where the old *IG* I, II, and
III have been superseded, to Epidaurus (*IG* IV² I), and to Aetolia and
Acarnania (*IG* IX² I), and it is already arguable that *IG* I², published
as long ago as 1924, is itself in need of a complete re-edition.

The volumes of *Inscriptiones Graecae*, however, extend only to
Europe. For Asia Minor, the Levant, Egypt and North Africa the
situation is much more complex and the material much less easily to be
located. No such unified publication exists, although a beginning has
been made, under Austrian leadership, of a series entitled *Tituli Asiae
Minoris*, so far confined to the inscriptions of Lycia but ultimately of
wider scope.[4] Otherwise it remains necessary to cite material from the
old Boeckh *Corpus*, from *MAMA* or other topographical studies as far
back as Le Bas and Waddington's *Voyage archéologique*, or from the
excavation reports of selected areas, which will be considered separately
later. Apart from *TAM* beginnings have been made on other *Corpus*-
like undertakings; some of these, such as *Studia Pontica*, vol. III, do
not go far, but others, such as *Inscriptions grecques et latines de la*

Syrie (*IGLS*), under the auspices of the French Institute of Archaeology at Beirut, Lebanon, create from the ground up a *Corpus* for the area with which they deal. For Egypt one may refer to the *Sammelbuch Griechischer Urkunden* (*SB*), for Tripolitania to the *Inscriptions of Roman Tripolitania* of J. M. Reynolds and J. B. Ward Perkins (restricted, however, in its content of Greek material).[5] Other material may be listed in the publications by individual museums already referred to. Much Egyptian material, for example, is in fact best to be found that way, in the catalogues of the museums at Alexandria and Cairo, while the *British Museum Inscriptions* contains many inscriptions from the coast of Asia Minor acquired by early archaeological adventures, which have now found their home in London. Mostly, however, epigraphic material from the eastern Greek world is to be found in the isolated articles of individual scholars published here and there among the learned journals, or united in separate undertakings such as the series published by Louis and Jeanne Robert under the title *Hellenica* and the many publications of such scholars as W. H. Buckler or Sir William Ramsay. Thus the problem of finding the 'definitive' edition of an inscription varies greatly according to whether it was discovered to the east of the Aegean or not, and, while many inscriptions from Asia Minor and farther east have been incorporated into 'Type-collections' or other such documentary compilations of material, they still lack an adequate term of reference such as those provided by *CIG* and *IG*, and it remains impossible to have at hand all the material from a given city or area, which is the principal blessing conferred, for Greece and western Europe, by the great German undertakings.

It may be suggested as a fundamental characteristic of a *Corpus* that it will contain a minimum of commentary and exegesis, for which it is content to abbreviate the essentials, or even merely to cite the reference, of the original publication of the stone and important discussions of it in the intervening years. This same brevity holds good even if material is being inserted into the *Corpus* for the first time. A *Corpus* is not the place for long comment and involved argument. A good modern example is that of W. Peek's *Griechische Vers-Inschriften*, in which the volumes of texts keep commentary and explanation within strict limits; the author's own discussions of both the old and the new material in his *Corpus* are properly reserved for a separate volume. On the whole, the 'type-collections' already discussed begin to depart from the character of a *Corpus* in that they extend the amount of discussion or include the inscriptions within the setting of a full-scale study of a particular subject. The same is true even of some volumes now included in the *IG* framework itself: *Inscriptiones Creticae*, a work taking the place of the unpublished *IG* XIII, contains an amount of commentary and *testimonia* which, useful though it is, far outdoes anything hitherto reckoned as essential for a *Corpus* volume.

If the 'Type-collection' and the 'Corpus-with-commentary' exist as developments of, and complements to, the basic and laconic *Corpus* on the geographical pattern, a further by-product has been the 'Digest-type' publication, selecting from the wealth of material available in the whole collection those texts which are likely to be of the greatest interest to the student primarily concerned with a specific period or topic. This genus differs from the 'Type-collection' in that it aims to be only selective, and not to collect *all* the material of a given character. As with the other classes, the amount of commentary included will vary. In some, such as V. Ehrenberg and A. H. M. Jones' *Documents to illustrate the reigns of Augustus and Tiberius*, where epigraphic material takes its place beside the evidence of coins and papyri, commentary is minimal. So also, for the most part, in R. Cagnat's *Inscriptiones Graecae ad res Romanas pertinentes* (*IGRR*) and C. Michel's *Recueil d'inscriptions grecques*, while W. Dittenberger's *Sylloge Inscriptionum Graecarum* (*Syll.* or *SIG*) and *Orientis Graeci Inscriptiones Selectae* (*OGIS* or *OGI*) content themselves with rather limited explanation of the matters they illustrate. Of the type of work aiming not only to provide a selection of useful inscriptions but also to use them as a basis for a brief but adequate commentary, M. N. Tod's *Greek Historical Inscriptions* may stand as perhaps the most characteristic and most frequently used representative. The works so far mentioned have aimed largely to provide a selection of material to illustrate problems of historical and social development. E. Schwyzer's *Dialectorum Graecarum Exempla Epigraphica* (*DGE*) selects inscriptions in much the same way for linguistic purposes. The system on which the material is arranged in these selective works is most usually chronological; but in some cases the chronological order is subordinated to geography (*IGRR*, *DGE*) and in others to a subdivision based on subject-matter and content (Ehrenberg–Jones, *Documents*). Dittenberger's *Sylloge* combines the two systems in that its last section is drawn up on the basis of subject-matter, while the earlier parts were strictly chronological in arrangement. In any case, as with the *Corpus* itself, chronology is always the basis of arrangement within the sections of a work of this kind, even where it does not form the basis of the work as a whole.

As a final addition to this series of 'Corpus-type' publications it is necessary to include the epigraphical volumes attached to, or the epigraphy worked into, the publications of archaeological excavations at a given site. Here the epigraphy is published as a purely archaeological find, and is often arranged not according to its date or its content but according to the part of the site at which it was discovered, as in the series *Fouilles de Delphes*. Sometimes a volume of the excavations' final publication is devoted to the epigraphy separately, as in the case of the *Inschriften von Olympia* and the *Inschriften von Pergamon*. Priene and Magnesia-on-the-Maeander have also had their inscriptions edited and published separately. The publication of Miletus is unusual in attempting to combine the two systems, but in cases where the epigraphy is worked into the overall account of the site it is more difficult to locate a required inscription and to refer to it conveniently when it has been located. Indeed, there comes a point at which this class begins to merge into that already discussed as 'Theme-publications', if the new material is included, perhaps along with the old, in a general discussion of the area and is integrated into the whole account of the findings of the expedition, as is the case with L. and J. Robert's *La Carie II*, on the Tabae and Heraclea Salbace area of south-western Anatolia. It is to be expected, however, that all newly discovered inscriptions published in this way will in due course be incorporated into any definitive *Corpus* which may eventually cover the area concerned. The *Corpus* publication, where it exists, always remains the fundamentally necessary citation for every text.

The supplementary publications. The problem for the average scholar, once he has found the *Corpus* reference for his text or has run to earth whatever is the basic publication of the inscription he is concerned with, is next that of discovering what work has been done subsequently towards the improvement of the original edition or its alinement with other knowledge on the subject with which it deals. It is obviously impossible for him to thumb through every likely publication during the intervening years in which some treatment of or reference to the stone in question may have occurred—an enormous labour of uncertain accuracy and result. Apart from full-scale books which he would have to consult, there are some two hundred periodicals and occasional publications concerned with classical matters, with an annual output of considerable proportions. The impasse is resolved by the existence of publications which give him the information he requires in a brief and easily accessible form. Between 1906 and 1955 M. N. Tod issued, at first in *The Year's Work in Classical Studies* and later in the *Journal of Hellenic Studies*, a series of Progress Reports, listing within the space of a few dozen pages references and notes on epigraphical publications appearing during the period, usually of two years, which he reviewed, in so far as they had come to his notice. The *Revue des études grecques* has for many years included an annual *Bulletin épigraphique*, latterly edited by the Roberts, which, for the purposes with which this section is concerned, gives the student a wide coverage of material and for the most part provides some idea of the substance of the articles reviewed, especially if they are not generally accessible. Neither of these publications has the space to quote to any significant extent the new or emended texts in their full detail, and the scholar who consults them cannot avoid turning to the publication they review, if he can find it. On the other hand this labour is saved for those who may not require to undertake it by the successive volumes of the *Supplementum Epigraphicum Graecum*; these now appear annually and reprint the entire texts of newly published material unless the new publication is itself a *Corpus* or a work of the same character. By listing its material with a volume and reference number in the same way as does the *Corpus* itself, *SEG* can serve, as its name suggests, as a running supplement to the volumes of the *Corpus*. While none of these works can presume to include all epigraphic material from whatever source, since much depends on the availability of the publications and the general co-operation of the scholarly world, it may on the whole be claimed that the researcher who has consulted all of them may rest assured that he has done what he can to discover the information that he needs. Progress Reports similar to those which Tod wrote for the *Journal of Hellenic Studies* exist also for more restricted fields. Tod himself, from 1913 to 1949, compiled such a report for the *Journal of Egyptian Archaeology* in respect of material discovered in or relating to Greco-Roman Egypt, continued since 1949 along the same lines by P. M. Fraser. A report on epigraphic studies relating to legal matters compiled by Alvaro D'Ors appears in *Studia et Documenta Historiae et Iuris* (cf. *SEG* XIII 624). Greek inscriptions concerned with Roman affairs find a supplement to *IGRR* in the annual publication on Latin Epigraphy, *L'Année épigraphique*, issued both as a separate publication and as part of the *Revue archéologique*. Finally, references to epigraphic publications are included in the general bibliographies of classical publications, of which the best known is that of J. Marouzeau published under the title *L'Année philologique*; others appear as supplements to periodicals such as *Gnomon* or the *Jahrbuch* of the German Archaeological Institute, or in reviews of the whole archaeological field such as *Fasti Archaeologici*. The epigraphic sections of these tend to be limited, as the field which they have to cover is so wide, and the arrangement by author's name, which they usually follow, is less helpful than the geographical system on the pattern of the *Corpus*, which is followed by the major publications of epigraphic material by itself listed earlier.

It may be, however, that a researcher really does not know where to start in his quest, or what are the basic publications on a given area or a given type of inscription which he ought to consult. He may not know, without looking it up, to which part of Greece a certain volume of *IG* refers, or to what author he should turn for material on, say, Mithraism or *defixiones*, medicine or temple-finance, or any other of the numerous headings under which the subject-matter of Greek inscriptions could, as we have seen, be arranged. In the appendix to his Introduction to Greek Epigraphy, to which he gave the title *Saxa Loquuntur*, J. J. E. Hondius aimed to provide just this kind of information. In upwards of one hundred pages he gives a succinct account of the principal *Hilfsmittel* for epigraphists, as it stood at the time at which he wrote (1938), arranged geographically, under museum-headings, and by subject. The two decades since then have, despite the long years of war and uncertainty, produced a great quantity of epigraphic work, and a major need of the present time is that Hondius' useful guide should be brought fully up to date. But it nevertheless remains a source of the most ready and valuable information on problems of this kind, and, using the bases which it provides, together with the assistance of the Progress Reports and of the *Supplementum Epigraphicum Graecum*, the scholar should find the path to the information he requires made relatively smooth.

APPENDIX TO CHAPTER IX

THE VOLUMES OF 'INSCRIPTIONES GRAECAE'

IG I   *Inscriptiones Atticae Euclidis anno vetustiores* (1873, with supplements appearing from 1877 to 1903). Originally known as *Corpus Inscriptionum Atticarum* I (with supplement in IV, 1). Superseded by

IG I²   *Inscriptiones Atticae Euclidis anno anteriores* (1924). For supplements to this volume see *SEG* III 1–67, X, XII 1–83, XIII 1–37, XIV 1–33, XV 1–82, *Athenian Tribute Lists*, vols. I–II.

IG II   *Inscriptiones Atticae aetatis quae est inter Euclidis annum et Augusti tempora* (in five parts, 1877–95). Originally known as *Corpus Inscriptionum Atticarum* II (with supplement in IV, 2).

IG III   *Inscriptiones Atticae aetatis Romanae* (in two parts, 1878–82, with an appendix in part 3, 1897). Originally known as *Corpus Inscriptionum Atticarum* III. Both *IG* II and *IG* III are now superseded by

IG II² (sometimes referred to as *IG* II/III²) *Inscriptiones Atticae Euclidis anno posteriores* (in four parts, 1913–40). For supplements to these volumes see, in addition to the bibliography given by Hondius, *Saxa Loquuntur* 68, *SEG* XII 84–215, XIII 38–225, XIV 34–296, XV 83–184. Part 1 of *IG* II² contains public decrees, part 2 catalogues, leases, etc., part 3 dedications, *tituli honorarii*, and (in the second section) funerary inscriptions. The archon lists in part IV have been replaced by later work on the subject, for which see Chapter X.

IG IV *Inscriptiones Argolidis* (1902). Originally known as *Corpus Inscriptionum Graecarum Peloponnesi et insularum vicinarum* I. For supplements to this volume see *SEG* I 64–80, II 52–8, III 309–19, XI 1–391, XIII 226–50, XIV 297–325, XV 185–204. The section dealing with Epidaurus has been superseded by

IG IV² part 1 *Inscriptiones Epidauri* (1929). For supplements to this volume see *SEG* XI 392–453, XIII 251–4, XIV 326–8, XV 205–14.

IG V part 1 *Inscriptiones Laconiae et Messeniae* (1913). For supplements to this volume see M. N. Tod, *BSA* XXVI (1923–5), 106–15, *SEG* I 81–91, II 59–179, III 320–2, XI 454–1041, XII 371, XIII 255–69, XIV 329–45, XV 215–26.

IG V part 2 *Inscriptiones Arcadiae* (1913). For supplements to this volume see *SEG* I 92–3, II 180–1, III 323–6, XI 1042–1169, XII 371, XIII 270–1, XIV 346–8, XV 227–40.

IG VI (*Inscriptiones Elidis et Achaiae*). This volume was never compiled. As a substitute it is necessary to refer to the publication of the inscriptions from Olympia in *Die Inschriften von Olympia* (1896) and to *SEG* I 94–7, II 182–3, III 327–9, XI 1170–1281, XII 216, 371, XIII 272, XIV 302, 349–77, XV 241–61, as well as to the bibliography in Hondius, *Saxa Loquuntur* 69–70.

IG VII *Inscriptiones Megaridis et Boeotiae* (1892). Originally known as *Corpus Inscriptionum Graecarum Graeciae Septentrionalis* I. For supplements to this volume see *SEG* I 98–143, II 184–253, III 333–77, XII 372, XIII 280–350, XIV 378–88, XV 262–335. Between 1930 and 1952 no Megarian or Boeotian material was included in *SEG*; material from the Megarid for those years is collected in *SEG* XIII, *loc. cit.* That from Boeotia should be sought from M. N. Tod's Progress Reports and other references.

IG VIII (*Inscriptiones Delphorum*). This volume has never been undertaken. It is necessary to consult the publications of the French excavators at Delphi, in particular vol. III of *Fouilles de Delphes* and the epigraphic material in the *Bulletin de Correspondance Hellénique*. See also *SEG* I 144–211, II 254–351, III 378–405, XII 217–65, XIII 351–81, XIV 389–466, XV 336–49; the years from 1930 to 1952 are not covered by *SEG*.

IG IX part 1 *Inscriptiones Phocidis, Locridis, Aetoliae, Acarnaniae, insularum maris Ionii* (1897). Originally known as *Corpus Inscriptionum Graecarum Graeciae Septentrionalis* III, i. The Aetolian and Acarnanian sections of this volume have been superseded by

IG IX² parts 1–2 *Inscriptiones Aetoliae* (1932) and *Inscriptiones Acarnaniae*

(1957). For supplements to these volumes see *SEG* XII 266–303, 377, XIII 384–5, XIV 467–72, XV 350–66; the years from 1932 to 1952 are not covered by *SEG*.

IG IX part 2 *Inscriptiones Thessaliae* (1908). For supplements to this volume see the bibliography of Hondius, *Saxa Loquuntur* 71, as well as *SEG* XII 304–10, XIII 386–96, XIV 473–4, XV 367–82, and (between 1930 and 1952) references in the Progress Reports and elsewhere.

IG X (*Inscriptiones Epiri, Macedoniae, Thraciae, Scythiae*). This volume has never been undertaken, although work is proceeding on the Macedonian section of it. Material from northern Greece and the Balkans is scattered and difficult of access. The long bibliography in Hondius, *Saxa Loquuntur* 72–6, is fundamental. It may be supplemented from the Progress Reports and from *SEG* XII 311–55, 373–6, XIII 397–417, XIV 475–89, XV 383–489 (from 1952 onwards). For inscriptions of the Russian shore of the Black Sea see B. Latyschev, *Inscriptiones antiquae orae septentrionalis Ponti Euxini Graecae et Latinae* in two volumes with supplement (1885–1901), the first of which was reworked in an improved second edition (1916). For Bulgaria see G. Mihailov, *Inscriptiones Graecae in Bulgaria repertae* (vol. I, 1956).

IG XI *Inscriptiones Deli* (1912–14). Only parts 2 and 4 of this volume were published. The remaining Delian inscriptions have been edited in a *Corpus*-form by the French excavators of Delos under the title *Inscriptions de Délos*, which renders further volumes of this section of *IG* unnecessary. For supplements see the Progress Reports, articles in the *Bulletin de Correspondance Hellénique*, and (since 1952) *SEG* XII 356–9, XIII 418–30, XIV 490–505, XV 490–5.

IG XII *Inscriptiones maris Aegaei praeter Delum*. This is subdivided into nine sections, which must be dealt with separately. Not all of the sections have been published. A supplement to sections 2, 3, 5, 7–9, usually referred to as *IG* XII Suppl., appeared in 1939.

IG XII part 1 *Inscriptiones Rhodi, Chalces, Carpathi cum Saro, Casi* (1895). For supplements to this volume see Hondius, *Saxa Loquuntur* 78, *SEG* XII 359a–365, XIII 431–2, XIV 506–15, XV 496–505, G. Pugliese Carratelli, *Supplemento Epigrafico Rodio*, in the *Annuario della Scuola Archeologica di Atene (Nuova Serie)*, XIV–XVI (1952–4), 247–316, I. Pugliese Carratelli and M. Segre, *Tituli Camirenses*, in the same *Annuario* XI–XIII (1949–51), 141–318, with additions in XIV–XVI (1952–4), 211–46, Chr. Blinkenberg, *Lindos* II (1941).

IG XII part 2 *Inscriptiones Lesbi, Nesi, Tenedi* (1899). For supplements to this volume see, besides Hondius, *Saxa Loquuntur* 78, and the Progress Reports, *SEG* XIII 433–9, XIV 516–17.

IG XII part 3 *Inscriptiones Symes, Teutlussae, Teli, Nisyri, Astypalaeae, Anaphes, Therae et Therasiae, Pholegandri, Cimoli, Meli* (1898–1904). Supplemented by *SEG* I 343, II 498–9, III 713–39, XII 366–7, XIII 440, XIV 518–23, XV 506–7, as well as by *IG* XII Suppl. and the Progress Reports.

IG XII part 4 (*Inscriptiones Coi et Calymni*). This section was never published. For Calymnos see M. Segre's *Tituli Calymnii* in the *Annuario della Scuola Archeologica di Atene* (*Nuova Serie*), VI–VII (1944–5) (*SEG* XII 386). For Cos see the bibliography of Hondius, *Saxa Loquuntur* 79, the Progress Reports, and (since 1952) *SEG* XII 368–85, XIII 441–3, XIV 524–9, XV 508–13.

IG XII part 5 *Inscriptiones Cycladum* (1903–9). For supplements see *IG* XII Suppl., Hondius, *Saxa Loquuntur* 79, the Progress Reports, and (since 1952) *SEG* XIII 444–51, XIV 530–55, XV 514–24.

IG XII part 6 (*Inscriptiones Chii et Sami*). This section was never published. See Hondius, *Saxa Loquuntur* 79, the Progress Reports, and (since 1952) *SEG* XII 387–93, XIII 452, XIV 556–64, XV 525–47.

IG XII part 7 *Inscriptiones Amorgi et insularum vicinarum* (1908). For additional material see *IG* XII Suppl., the Progress Reports, and (since 1952) *SEG* XIII 453–5, XV 548–9.

IG XII part 8 *Inscriptiones insularum maris Thracici* (1909). For additional material see *IG* XII Suppl., the Progress Reports, *SEG* I 407–8, II 504–8, III 753–7, XII 394–9, XIII 456–61, XIV 565–72, XV 550–6, J. Pouilloux, *Recherches sur l'histoire et les cultes de Thasos* I (1954).

IG XII part 9 *Inscriptiones Euboeae insulae* (1915). For additional material see *IG* XII Suppl., the Progress Reports, and *SEG* I 409, III 758–73, XII 400–1, XIII 462, XIV 573–5, XV 557–63.

IG XIII (*Inscriptiones Creticae*). This section of *IG* has never been published, but its place has been taken by an Italian publication, edited by Margherita Guarducci, to which the same name was given. This includes in four volumes, published over the years 1935–50, all Cretan inscriptions of certain provenience with a full commentary. For additional bibliography see Hondius, *Saxa Loquuntur* 80, the Progress Reports, and *SEG* XII 402–4, XIII 463–8, XIV 576–9, XV 564–77.

IG XIV *Inscriptiones Siciliae et Italiae, additis Graecis Galliae, Hispaniae, Britanniae, Germaniae inscriptionibus* (1890). Material of later date is widely scattered in various periodicals, particularly those of Italy. The volumes of *Inscriptiones Italiae*, a new Italian *Corpus*-publication of which fascicules appear from time to time, include Greek as well as Latin material. Greek inscriptions from Isola Sacra near Ostia appear in H. Thylander's *Inscriptions du Port d'Ostie* (1952). See, however, Hondius, *Saxa Loquuntur* 81, the Progress Reports, and (since 1952) *SEG* XII 405–17, XIII 469–86, XIV 580–637, XV 578–630.

(J. J. E. Hondius, *Saxa Loquuntur* 67–81, gives in greater detail the information included here, as it stood in 1938 when he wrote: a summary list is also to be found in G. Klaffenbach's *Griechische Epigraphik*, 21–7, which also includes references to other collections of inscriptions given in a fuller form by Hondius, *op. cit.* 82–101.)

CHAPTER X

SOME MISCELLANEOUS INFORMATION

A STUDENT of the classics, challenged suddenly to name the Nine Muses, or to identify the Seven Sages, or to give a list of the Seven Wonders of the World, might find himself hard put to it to provide the answers without turning to some book of reference. And even then he might not be too sure in what context he could lay his hands on the information required. In much the same way, the student of Greek epigraphy—and especially of Attic epigraphy, on which this book has set its main emphasis—frequently finds himself in need of simple information without having it readily to hand or being aware of the references to which he should turn. Where quickly to find, for instance, a list of the Athenian archons of the fifth century, or a table of Greek numerals, or how to make certain whether the month Maimakterion came before or after Gamelion? Some people do, no doubt, carry this sort of thing in their heads. They will justly scorn this final chapter; it is not for them. It seeks only to collect together some of the varied information of this kind, and to put it in one place where a scholar knows that it is available if he wants it. The selection is arbitrary, and is geared to the assumption that information on Attic epigraphy is what the majority of the users of this book are, in the first place, likely to require. But there is a great deal more that might have been included from other parts of the Greek world, and it is no bad suggestion that a notebook of such miscellanea, ready to hand on the shelf, is one of the most useful compilations a student can make for himself, shaped around his own particular interests. Or at the least, if it is true that the wise man is not the man who knows, but the man who knows where to find out, a list of vital references in a handy place can save precious time in a crisis.

The numerals. Not many would trust themselves to write without hesitation in Greek numbers a figure such as 1066, whether in the alphabetic or the acrophonic numeral system, let alone in both. To consult a table of the numerals, and to work it out from that, is the safest and quickest way. The numerical systems have been the subject of comprehensive study by M. N. Tod, embodied in a series of articles in the *Annual* of the British School of Archaeology at Athens,[1] and to these the reader may be referred for a full discussion of the question in detail and for a review of the evidence and of the varying forms used. Of the two systems, that called the *acrophonic* is earlier in date, and may be considered first. As its name implies, all that it involves is the use of the initial letter of the word by which the number is called, to represent the number itself. For instance, Γ (i.e. πέντε)=5, Δ (i.e. δέκα)=10, Η (i.e. *h*εκατόν)=100. The exception to this general rule is the unit, 1, which is represented by a simple upright stroke. Numbers for 50, 500, and 5000 are arrived at by a combination of the signs for 10, 100, and 1000 with that for 5. The '5' sign has a small version of the number by which it is multiplied as it were suspended from it; thus Γ^Δ represents 50, a combination of 5 and 10, Γ^Η 500, and Γ^Χ (Γ plus Χ (χίλιοι))=5000. The other numbers, apart from Μ (10,000), are compounded of these basic elements, the required figures being set beside one another in such a way that the largest figure comes first. For example, 6 is represented by a 5 plus a 1, Γ plus Ι, i.e. ΓΙ: 16 will be ΔΓΙ, 66 Γ^ΔΔΓΙ. 2 is shown simply by two units, set side by side, 20 by two 'tens', and so forth. 1066 will thus appear as a combination of 1000, 50, 10, 5 and 1: ΧΓ^ΔΔΓΙ.[2]

Inscriptions involving money use these same figures with slight changes. It is of course readily apparent from the context when the numeration represents a monetary total, and on financial inscriptions recognisable as such there is no special indication or introduction for the figure as constituting drachmae rather than anything else. On inscriptions of other types, where an amount of money is suddenly introduced, the word δραχμαί or an abbreviation of it, or in later times δηνάρια or its abbreviation *, will be included, as in example 25 at the end of Chapter IV. The major variation is that a single drachma is shown as ⊢. The unit sign Ι is used to represent one obol. Where talents are concerned, the single acrophonic Τ represents one talent: five, ten, and higher numbers of talents combine the Τ with the number concerned and write Γ^Τ, ⊿, Η̵, etc. 50 talents need a combination of Γ, Δ, and Τ, and produce the hybrid sign Γ^Τ. The same system may be applied, in place of talents, to staters (ϛ). As an example, ΤΤΧΧΗΔΔ⊢⊢ represents 2 talents 2122 drachmae.

This acrophonic system is best attested in Attica, where the earliest example (in the tribute lists) belongs to the middle of the fifth century. But according to Herodian[3] numerals of this kind occurred in the written record of Solon's legislation, and there is little doubt that it is the older of the Greek numerical systems, with an origin perhaps as early as the seventh century. The table which follows gives a specimen list of the Attic signs. The scattered evidence from other places follows the Attic 'norm' in general, but a number of variants occur, some of them not consistent with the acrophonic principle. For these it is best to consult M. N. Tod's full account: but it may be worth mentioning here that M may in some cases represent one mina rather than the figure 10,000, that C (half-obol in Attic) represents the unit 1 at Troezen, and that T (1 talent) may also stand for a quarter-obol (τεταρτημόριον). For non-Attic numerical notation a good example to turn to is that of the building records of the fourth century from Epidaurus (*IG* IV² 1,102–120; cf. *SEG* XI 416, 417, 417*a*), in which a system of dots and dashes is combined with the acrophonic system, and a drachma is shown as ·, with ten drachmae as -. But it is essential to become familiar with the standard signs before adventuring on these and other variants and refinements.

The acrophonic system declined before the competition of the less cumbersome alphabetic: it may still be found in the first century B.C., and Tod believes also that the classicism of the Hadrianic age perpetuated it in at least one instance. The evidence suggests, however, that inscriptions showing this type of numeration are not likely, unless special reasons can be adduced, to be datable later than *c.* 100 B.C.

I = 1	ΔΔ = 20	HH = 200
II = 2	ΔΔΓ = 25	Γ⁼ = 500
III = 3	ΔΔΔ = 30	Γ⁼HH = 700
IIII = 4	Γ⁼ = 50	Γ⁼HHΓI = 706
Γ = 5	Γ⁼Γ = 55	X = 1000
ΓI = 6	Γ⁼Δ = 60	XX = 2000
ΓII = 7	Γ⁼ΔΔI = 71	Γ⁼ = 5000
Δ = 10	H = 100	M = 10,000
ΔII = 12	HΔ = 110	MM = 20,000
ΔΓ = 15	HΔI = 111	
ΔΓI = 16	HΓ⁼ = 150	

MMΓ⁼XXΓ⁼HΓ⁼ΔΔΓIII = 27,678

C = ½ obol	I = 1 obol	⊢ = 1 drachma
T = 1 talent	Γ⁼ = 5 talents	⋌ = 10 talents
⋌⋌ = 20 talents	H = 100 talents	X = 1000 talents
Γ⁼ = 50 talents		

⋌⋌TTXΓ⁼HΓ⁼Δ⊢⊢II = 22 tal. 1662 dr. 2 obols

6 obols = 1 drachma   100 drachmae = 1 mina

6000 drachmae = 1 talent

{ = 1 stater   Γ⁼ = 5 staters   ⋌ = 10 staters

In the Athenian Tribute Lists the amounts shown against the names of the cities are not those of the total tribute paid but of the one-sixtieth of the full amount which was given as an ἀπαρχή to Athena. Thus a figure of ⟨Ϥ⟩ represents 50 drachmae paid as the ἀπαρχή-quota; the amount of tribute it reflects will be 50×60, i.e. 3000 drachmae, or XXX. Other frequently occurring quotas are ΓⱵⱵΙΙ (8 dr. 2 obols), which represents a tribute of 500 drachmae, ΔΓⱵΙΙΙΙ (16 dr. 4 obols), a tribute of 1000 drachmae, ΔΔΔⱵⱵΙΙ (33 dr. 2 obols), a tribute of 2000 drachmae, and Η (100 drachmae), which is the quota for a talent of tribute. For a complete table of the tribute equivalents of the quotas entered in the lists see *The Athenian Tribute Lists*, vol. II (1949), pp. 122–4. A table in Arabic figures of actual amounts paid or believed to have been paid as tribute during the period of the Pentekontaetia is provided in G. F. Hill, *Sources for Greek History between the Persian and Peloponnesian Wars* (ed. 2, 1951, rev. R. Meiggs and A. Andrewes), pp. 404–23.

The *alphabetic* system has the merits of brevity and simplicity. It can express high numbers in a short series of three or four letters instead of a long compendium of side-by-side addition such as that illustrated above; and it makes use of the letters of the alphabet in their well-known order without recourse, save in the case of 900, to novelties. It is well described by Tod in the last of the series of articles referred to in note 1, a description which any short account can do no more than paraphrase. The first nine letters of the alphabet (α to θ, since *digamma* is included) represent the numbers 1 to 9, the next nine letters (ι to *koppa*) represent 10 to 90, and ρ to ω fill out the remainder from 100 to 800. This left, in the hundreds series, 900 unprovided for, and this was represented by a letter which we call *sampi*, but which was probably derived ultimately from the unused sibilant *tsade* (see above, p. 15). The forms of this letter vary, but it is usually shown as something like ↑ or ⟩. For the thousands, the series begins again with the same letters as those used for the units, α to θ, prefixed to the complex but normally with some mark, such as a preceding stroke, to indicate that these letters are here representing thousands. Thus the example 1066 will appear in the alphabetic system as /ΑΖϝ, three letters with a stroke in front of the initial *alpha* to show that it stands here for 1000. For ten thousand and above, the acrophonic M for μύριοι continued to be used, with a small letter above it to show what multiple of ten thousand is in question, and also to differentiate it from the M which represents 40. Thus M̆=10,000, M̆=20,000, and so on. As with the acrophonic system, the number normally reads from left to right, from the highest element in the complex to the smallest. Occasionally, in numbers below 1000, a reverse order may be met with: this is in fact not uncommon outside Attica, but in Attic epigraphy it is a rarity.[4]

It was a general practice, with acrophonic as well as with alphabetic numerals, to distinguish the letters used for numerical purposes from the rest of the inscription either by leaving a blank space on the inscription before and after them, or by inserting some mark of punctuation. Sometimes a sign, such as a horizontal line, is added above the numeral, and this may be used with or without the punctuation marks, which are on the same level as the numeral. The punctuation mark may be no more than a simple dot or pair of dots, but it may, especially in Hellenistic and Roman times, take a more fancy form, such as an ivy leaf. The two-dotted colon is indeed often associated with acrophonic numerals, as is a variant with three dots, but seems not to be used with their alphabetic counterparts.

The earliest use of the alphabetic system seems to have been less as actual numbers than as labels, to distinguish clauses of a document or items in an inventory, in much the same way as (*a*), (*b*), (*c*), etc., are used at the present time.[5] Such a use is already found in the fifth century.[6] But the evidence for alphabetic numerals as such seems not to antedate the second century, and is more familiar as a phenomenon of the Christian era. The system continued in use to the end of the Roman Empire and into the Byzantine period.

The table of alphabetic numerals which follows omits the marks customarily used in modern texts to draw attention to the fact that numbers are involved. These usually take the form of a mark *above* the line, like an acute accent ('), *following* numbers up to 999, and, in the case of numbers of 1000 and above, a similar mark in addition, *below* the line and *preceding* the numeral. For example, 555 is customarily shown as φνε', 5555 as ,εφνε'.

α=1	ι=10	ρ=100
β=2	κ=20	σ=200
γ=3	λ=30	τ=300
δ=4	μ=40	υ=400
ε=5	ν=50	φ=500
ϝ=6	ξ=60	χ=600
ϡ=7	ο=70	ψ=700
η=8	π=80	ω=800
θ=9	ϟ=90	ϡ=900

The Athenian tribes. Among the reforms introduced into the Athenian constitution by Cleisthenes in 508/7 B.C., after the expulsion of the Pisistratidae and the party strife which followed it, was one by which ten new tribes were substituted, as part of the machinery of government, for the traditional four. These new tribes were named after Attic heroes, the names chosen by the Pythia at Delphi from among a selection submitted to her. The records show that, once established, these ten tribes had an official and permanent order in which they were listed, although it is quite uncertain how this order arose. It appears in a variety of connexions—for example on official casualty lists, in which the fallen are shown, tribe by tribe, set out in the recognised order of tribal names. It also appears, reflected in public decrees and the like, in the rotation of certain official duties, such as the secretaryship of the *boule*, in which W. S. Ferguson was the first to observe a recurrent pattern of secretaries selected from each tribe in turn, in the official order of the tribes—a pattern which has, as a result, become generally known as 'Ferguson's Law'.[7] The usefulness of this law for a study of the calendar and in fixing the dates of the archons who gave their names to the Attic years is immeasurable. It establishes, for instance, that two archons each with a secretary of the *boule* from the same tribe must be separated from one another by an interval of years equal to the number of the remainder of the tribes, or by that interval plus a multiple of the total number of tribes. That is, in the period when there were twelve tribes the interval between two archons having secretaries from the same tribe would be 11, or 23, or 35 years, and so on in the same progression. The ten Cleisthenic tribes, in their regular order, were the following:[8]

Erechtheis	I	Leontis	IV	Hippothontis	VIII
Aigeis	II	Akamantis	V	Aiantis	IX
Pandionis	III	Oineis	VI	Antiochis	X
		Kekropis	VII		

Cleisthenes divided the basic element of the Attic social and political structure, the demes, among these tribes in such a way that each tribe became roughly equal in the number of citizens it contained—not equal, however, in the number of demes which each comprehended, since the demes varied in their geographical size and in their population. His arrangements held good throughout the fifth and fourth centuries until the year 307/6 B.C., when two new tribes were added. They were designed to honour King Antigonus I Monophthalmos and his son Demetrius Poliorcetes for the 'liberation' of Athens from Macedonian control and the ten-year régime of Demetrius of Phalerum, and in consequence they received the names Antigonis and Demetrias. These two took their places at the head of the list, in front of Erechtheis, which then became tribe III, with Aigeis as tribe IV, and so on. This 'twelve-tribe system' continued in Athens for more than eighty years, until in 224/3 the Athenian policy of fostering close ties with the Ptolemaic kingdom in Egypt was reflected in the creation of a thirteenth tribe. This, like Antigonis and Demetrias, was made up of demes and fractions of demes removed from the tribes already existing, but in this case the Egyptian royal house received the additional honour of the creation of a new deme, named *Berenikidai*, after Berenice II, the wife of King Ptolemy III Euergetes. The new tribe, named Ptolemais, took its place between Leontis and Akamantis as the seventh in order,[9] and at this stage the 'official' tribal list was as follows:

Antigonis	I	Pandionis	V	Kekropis	X
Demetrias	II	Leontis	VI	Hippothontis	XI
Erechtheis	III	Ptolemais	VII	Aiantis	XII
Aigeis	IV	Akamantis	VIII	Antiochis	XIII
		Oineis	IX		

At the end of the century two events connected with the outbreak of the Second Macedonian War brought about further changes in the tribal arrangement. It remains in dispute what action it was, on the part of Philip V of Macedon, which so aroused the Athenians' anger that they abolished the two 'Macedonian' tribes, Antigonis and Demetrias, but the abolition took place, in 201–200 B.C., before the actual outbreak of war between Philip and the Athenians.[10] When that war did break out, the difficulties of Athens were greatly relieved by the prompt action of King Attalus I of Pergamum, in whose honour a new tribe Attalis was thereupon created and named. Thus a period of eleven tribes can have lasted at best only a few months, and from the year 200 onwards the twelve-tribe system was resumed, the place of Attalis being at the end of the list, after Antiochis.

No further changes took place until the second century A.D., when in 124/5 a thirteenth tribe was again added, this time to honour the philhellene Emperor Hadrian, whose benevolence to the city was so great and so tangibly demonstrated that such a notable recompense seemed more than justified. An assortment of demes was allocated to the new tribe, apparently on the principle of one deme from each existing tribe, although a new deme was also created for it, named after the Emperor's favourite, Antinous, in 130 after the latter's death. The new tribe was placed seventh in order, between Akamantis and Oineis, and the tribal list after A.D. 125 was therefore:

Erechtheis	I	Ptolemais	V	Hippothontis	X
Aigeis	II	Akamantis	VI	Aiantis	XI
Pandionis	III	Hadrianis	VII	Antiochis	XII
Leontis	IV	Oineis	VIII	Attalis	XIII
		Kekropis	IX		

The demes. To provide a complete list of the Attic demes, and to describe their division between the tribes as they stood at the various periods outlined above, would be beyond the compass of this chapter. Since the multiplicity of deme-names and the variety of the deme-assignments may be apt to confuse the unwary, it is however worth including a note at this point as to where a list of the demes may be found: most obviously, of course, in Pauly–Wissowa, *Realencyclopädie der classischen Altertumswissenschaft*, Band v, *s.v.* Δῆμοι, but also at the back of J. Kirchner's *Prosopographia Attica*. In both places their tribal attribution is also shown. W. K. Pritchett has published a special study of the rearrangement of the demes which took place on the creation of the new tribes, and this may be recommended to those who require fuller and more recent information on this point.[11] Pritchett has also observed[12] that *IG* II² 2362, an unfinished list of demes, reflects the speedy abandonment of the eleven-tribe system in 201–200 on the creation of Attalis. The geographical location of the demes, uncertain in a large number of cases and needing more precise definition in others, is to be the subject of a special study by C. W. J. Eliot.

The Athenian archons. As explained in Chapter v above, the archon-list at Athens between the Persian Wars and the end of the fourth century, i.e. until the record of Diodorus Siculus fails us, is well established, and the complete lists may be found in M. N. Tod's *Greek Historical Inscriptions*, vols. I and II, for the period from 500 to 323 B.C. For the 'Periclean' period see also G. F. Hill's *Sources for Greek history between the Persian and Peloponnesian Wars* (ed. 2, rev. R. Meiggs and A. Andrewes), 397–401. The archons of the archaic period are listed and discussed at length by T. J. Cadoux in the *Journal of Hellenic Studies* LXVIII (1948), 70–123. The archonships of the Hellenistic and Roman periods are still very much *sub judice*, and our knowledge of them depends on the survival of evidence in texts of the years in question, helped out by application of Ferguson's Law. The result is a complicated and interdependent framework which new discoveries have from time to time disrupted in a thoroughgoing way just as a satisfactory arrangement seemed to have been worked out. At present the list which is best to be recommended as a basis is that provided at the beginning of *The Chronology of Hellenistic Athens* (1940), by W. K. Pritchett and B. D. Meritt: but a substantial part of the list as there shown has come under revision, and new schemes have been published, first by W. B. Dinsmoor in *Hesperia* XXIII (1954), 312–16, and later by B. D. Meritt, *Hesperia* XXVI (1957), 94–7. It is to be hoped that further evidence and further discussion will in the end produce a reliable archon-list for Hellenistic Athens. In any event, some archon-ships, according to the nature of the evidence, must be regarded as fixed points, while others, even if perhaps to be dated elsewhere, cannot be altered so far as to remove them from the same general area in which they are now placed.

The application of Ferguson's Law to Athenian archons in the period of the Roman Empire has been particularly studied by J. A. Noto-poulos, and the reader may be referred for a detailed account to his two articles in the *American Journal of Philology* LXIV (1943), 44–55, and *Hesperia* XVIII (1949), 1–57. For the archons of the first century B.C., a period which also presents difficulty, see Sterling Dow, *American Journal of Archaeology* XXXVII (1933), 578–88, and *Hesperia*, Suppl. VIII (1949), 116–25.

The Athenian calendar.[13] The problems of the archonship bring us directly face to face with those of the calendar, the complexities of which are such that it is perhaps rash to attempt to give a brief outline of them. But since the calendar of Athens offers a major stumbling-block for those who have not immersed themselves thoroughly in the subject, and a continuing source of argument for those who have, such an attempt probably ought to be made. To judge from their official documents, the Athenians regularly made use of two calendaric systems, a reckoning by lunar months and a reckoning according to the boards of *prytaneis*, the subdivisions of the *boule* on a tribal basis which took it in turn to act as a standing committee of that body.[14] Each tribe 'held the prytany' for part of the term of office of the *boule* of the year; in the period of ten tribes, each tribe was in prytany for one-tenth of the year. The name of the tribe was chosen by lot as the term of its predecessor approached its end, and it was therefore not until the last-but-one tribe had been chosen that it was ever possible to know in advance the name of the tribe that would come next—by which time the process of elimination left no alternative.[15] Thus it was possible to give a date to a document, a decree of the *boule* and *demos* for instance, by saying that it was approved 'on the seventh day of the prytany of Aigeis, the sixth tribe in prytany'. In the fifth and early fourth century no further information was given. The first day of the first prytany regularly fell somewhere about 1 July in the Julian calendar, and from the beginning of the fourth century always coincided with the first day of the lunar calendar-year, 1 Hekatombaion. Aristotle tells us (*Constitution of Athens* 43) that the prytanies succeeded each other at regular intervals, the first four prytanies being of thirty-six days each and the last six of thirty-five. The total of 354 days equalled the total of the twelve months of the lunar calendar, which had six months of thirty days each and six of twenty-nine, known as 'full' (πλήρεις) and 'hollow' (κοῖλοι) months respectively. Aristotle's information relates to the period of ten tribes, and the periods subsequent to that time which saw twelve or thirteen tribes in existence also saw modifications in the arrangement of which he speaks. The intercalation of months and days in the lunar calendar, in order to bring it into line with the solar year when it became obviously out of step, also resulted in difficulties.

With an example such as that cited above, we may work out that the decree in question will have been passed on the 186th day of the conciliar (i.e. the prytany) year. Assuming for the moment that we are dealing, like Aristotle, with the period of ten tribes, this is the product of 4×36 days in the first four prytanies, plus 35 days in the fifth, plus 7 in the sixth. If the civil (i.e. the lunar) year began on the first day of the first prytany, and if there were no intercalations and nothing to disturb a regular succession of full and hollow months, the 186th day of the year would be, on the lunar reckoning, the ninth day of the seventh month, i.e. 9 Gamelion, and in our own terms, again assuming no complicating factor, would fall somewhere in early January. Unfortunately 'equations' between the conciliar and civil calendars, where they are inscribed on the documents, do not always attest such perfect regularity. They point in fact to a fluid system, in which the synchronisms of the two with regard to each other, and, in addition, of both vis-à-vis the solar year, were always running into trouble. Various efforts have been made to bring order out of chaos, although it may be suspected that modern scholarship, itself bred of a world dominated by the tyranny of the clock, may be demanding of the ancient world a precision which it neither had nor cared to acquire.

It has, for instance, been contended that in the later fifth century the Athenians adopted the nineteen-year astronomical cycle of Meton, which required intercalation of a month seven times during the period, and that this system formed their fixed basis, around which the conciliar calendar as it were revolved. Where the two calendars seem to fall out of line, it has usually proved possible to evade the difficulty or to emend the text. On the other hand, it has been proposed with equal conviction that the Metonic cycle is valueless as a basis for argument, and that the one regular and consistent element in Athenian time-reckoning was formed by the recurrent prytany-periods as described by Aristotle. The lunar calendar was, according to this argument, altered as required to fit with the conciliar year; and it is true that there is no sign in the evidence of regular intercalation such as a rigid adherence to the use of the Metonic cycle presupposes. In addition, there are instances in the second century B.C. in which the civil date is given according to a double reckoning, one κατὰ θεόν, which seems to be correct according to the lunar calendar, and another κατ' ἄρχοντα (always, in the examples, giving a date earlier than that 'according to the god') which seems to represent some arbitrary official tampering with the lunar date on a temporary basis, the difference being officially rectified when the occasion for it had passed. Such tampering is, again, always with the lunar calendar, which seems to imply that the conciliar calendar was the one which maintained the stricter regularity. But it must be admitted that to impose this form of regularity also demands some degree of assumption that a number of texts, as we have them, are incorrectly engraved. In fact, no system propounded hitherto is without its faults, and it may be suggested that none is likely to be forthcoming which will satisfy the tidy chronological taste of the present day.

It would be suspected, of course, that in the period of twelve tribes the prytany period and the lunar month would be coterminous, or very nearly so; but this is far from being the case, even in an ordinary and not an intercalary year. What is needed is a great deal more evidence of an explicit character; but unless or until this is available it is wiser to suspend judgement and remain content to note the possibilities already advanced.

In the meantime, some basic and agreed points may be set down as items of general usefulness:

1. The Attic months, in their order, were as follows:[16]

1. Hekatombaion	5. Maimakterion	9. Elaphebolion
2. Metageitnion	6. Posideion	10. Mounychion
3. Boedromion	7. Gamelion	11. Thargelion
4. Pyanopsion	8. Anthesterion	12. Skirophorion

2. The intercalary month was usually, though not invariably, a second Posideion, coming before Gamelion.

3. Hekatombaion 1st fell, theoretically, on the day of the new moon first after the summer solstice. But this rule of thumb cannot be relied upon, and exceptions are all too numerous. Hekatombaion 1st was the day on which the archons and other officials took office, and from the last decade of the fifth century onward was also the date on which the new *boule* came into office. But it should be borne in mind that during the Periclean and nearly all of the Peloponnesian War periods the *boule* of the new year might overlap slightly with the archon of the old year, or the old *boule* with the new archon. For a convenient table showing the archon and *boule* dates for this period, with the Julian equivalents, see B. D. Meritt, *Athenian Financial Documents* (1932), 176. The prytany year at that time was apparently of 366 days (six prytanies of thirty-seven days plus four of thirty-six), and existed as it were independently of the civil year, the Aristotelian arrangement not yet having been evolved. It is however fair to say that the evidence for the Athenian conciliar calendar of the fifth century is incomplete and still the subject of discussion: but it has been felt advisable to add something about it here, since it concerns a much studied period and is, in consequence, likely to present difficulties.

4. The sequence of full and hollow months was irregular in any given year, and it cannot be assumed that because one month had thirty days its successor and predecessor will have had twenty-nine.

5. The days according to the civil calendar were designated as three separate groups. For the first ten days the phraseology was of the 'rising' month: for example, Μεταγειτνιῶνος ἕκτη ἱσταμένου, on the sixth of Metageitnion. For the next ten days, the count was made with the formula 'plus ten', e.g., for the sixteenth of Metageitnion, Μεταγειτνιῶνος ἕκτη ἐπὶ δέκα. The last nine or ten days were however counted *backwards* from the end of the month, and designated either as of the 'waning' month (φθίνοντος) or as 'after the twenties' (μετ' εἰκάδας). Thus 26 Metageitnion would appear either as Μεταγειτνιῶνος πέμπτη φθίνοντος or as Μεταγειτνιῶνος πέμπτη μετ' εἰκάδας. The 29th would, in a hollow month, be counted as ἕνη καὶ νέα, and in a full month would be δευτέρα φθίνοντος or μετ' εἰκάδας. In the full month the 30th would take its place as ἕνη καὶ νέα.

The months at Delphi. Apart from the Attic calendar, that which the scholar is perhaps most liable to meet is that of Delphi, from which, as has been described elsewhere, the material is particularly rich. This, and other local calendars, are set out in Pauly–Wissowa, *Realencyclopädie*, s.v. *Kalender*, but the names and order of months in some localities are imperfectly known and the lists cannot be taken as definitive in all cases.[17] The Delphic year began roughly at the same time as that in Attica, but allowance must be made in either case for official interference. The months are listed in the same way as the Attic months above, beginning with the new year in July.

1. Ἀπελλαῖος	5. Δαιδαφόριος	9. Θεοξένιος
2. Βουκάτιος	6. Ποιτρόπιος	10. Ἐνδυσποιτρόπιος
3. Βοαθόος	7. Ἀμάλιος	11. Ἡράκλειος
4. Ἡραῖος	8. Βύσιος	12. Ἰλαῖος

As in Athens, the sixth month was generally repeated in an intercalary year.

The information here collected and compressed will, of course, be found in the references cited, set out at greater length and in greater detail. But to have it in one place, concisely stated, may be thought to have its own particular value, and the collection may be altered or augmented according to the special interests of the reader, for whom it should provide no more than a working basis for ready reference. Indeed, the aim of the whole volume may be described in much the same terms. Epigraphy is not the narrow discipline which the uninstructed sometimes allege that it is: it offers a rich harvest of study to the scholar at all stages of his development, touching as it does the whole range of Greek achievement. This book has been written in the hopes that these riches may be made available to a wider circle, and that an increasing number of classical scholars may find in Greek epigraphy a new and perhaps unsuspected field, to which they may feel encouraged to bring their own contributions and resources, and in which they will reap their own rewards of labour and discovery.

NOTES

INTRODUCTION

[1] Apart from Tod's survey in the *Oxford Classical Dictionary*, with which a valuable bibliography is also included, one might instance the section on Epigraphy by E. S. Roberts and E. A. Gardner contributed to the *Companion to Greek Studies* (ed. 4, 1931), that by F. Hiller von Gaertringen in the Gercke–Norden *Einleitung in die Altertumswissenschaft* (1 Band, 9 Heft), and that by A. Rehm in Otto's *Handbuch der Archäologie*. G. Klaffenbach's *Griechische Epigraphik* (1957) is of much the same size and scope as the present volume. E. S. Roberts' *Introduction to Greek Epigraphy* (vol. II with E. A. Gardner) has long been out of print, and its first volume is concerned wholly with the inscriptions of the archaic period, down to the end of the stage of the 'epichoric alphabets' which are studied in chapter II below. The most helpful and substantial handbook remains that of W. Larfeld, cited many times in this book, but its size and detail are more than the non-specialist might require, and a shorter survey is on that account not without point.

[2] 'Greek Epigraphy is the study of inscriptions written on durable material, such as stone or metal, in Greek letters and expressed in the Greek language. Coin-legends are regarded as falling within the province of the numismatist, painted mummy-labels and ink-written texts on ostraca (fragments of coarse pottery), specially numerous in and characteristic of Egypt, are claimed by the papyrologist, and painted inscriptions forming part of the original decoration of vases are assigned primarily to ceramics, though texts subsequently incised on pottery and the stamps on Rhodian and other amphorae are usually deemed epigraphical materials. The study covers an area coextensive with the lands inhabited or visited by Greeks who left behind written memorials, and a period of well over a millennium, from the appearance of the earliest extant examples of Greek writing down to the close of the fourth century or even later, when Greek merges into Byzantine history.'

[3] See L. Robert, *L'Épigraphie grecque au Collège de France* (1939), *Actes du deuxième congrès international d'épigraphie grecque et latine* (1952), 8–12; J. Pouilloux, *Des rapports actuels de l'épigraphie et de l'histoire grecques*, in *L'Antiquité Classique* XXII (1953), 32–49.

[4] *IG* I² 63. See the text in *The Athenian Tribute Lists* vol. II (1949), 40–3, where it is designated as A9.

CHAPTER I

[1] On what follows see also the remarks of G. Klaffenbach, *Griechische Epigraphik* (Göttingen, 1957), 99–100; W. Larfeld, *Griechische Epigraphik* (1914), §§127–31. On the Leiden system see U. Wilcken, *Archiv für Papyrusforschung* X (1933), 211–12; B. A. van Groningen, *Mnemosyne* (2nd Ser.),

LIX (1932), 362–5; J. J. E. Hondius, Introduction to *Supplementum Epigraphicum Graecum (SEG)* VII (1934).

² The Leiden system was severely though unjustifiably criticised by L. and J. Robert in *La Carie* II (1954), 9–13, and their remarks were in turn commented upon by G. Klaffenbach in *Gnomon* XXVII (1955), 239–40. No system is foolproof, but the Roberts chose as the principal target of their criticism a difficult and extreme case, nor was the system preferred by them any improvement on the Leiden symbols. The desirability of a uniform usage in any case outweighs such shortcomings as the Leiden system may have, and in cases of particular difficulty editors usually add an explanatory note to make the meaning of their textual indications quite clear.

³ The divergent use most often encountered at the present time is that of round brackets ( ) in cases where the Leiden system advocates the angled form ⟨ ⟩.

⁴ Used for example in such well-known textbooks as W. Dittenberger's *Sylloge Inscriptionum Graecarum (Syll.* or *SIG)*, ed. 3 (1915–24), and *Orientis Graeci Inscriptiones Selectae (OGIS)* (1903–5); M. N. Tod, *Greek Historical Inscriptions* I (ed. 2, 1946) and II (1948); V. Ehrenberg and A. H. M. Jones, *Documents illustrating the reigns of Augustus and Tiberius* (ed. 2, 1955).

⁵ See for example texts published in the *Bulletin de Correspondance Hellénique* and such works as J. Pouilloux's *La forteresse de Rhamnonte* and *Recherches sur l'histoire et les cultes de Thasos* I (1954).

⁶ On the abbreviations here used, and the *corpus* of Greek inscriptions in general, together with comparable collections of epigraphic material, see Chapter IX.

⁷ The same system holds good for letters barely legible for other reasons besides that quoted as an example, when stones are battered or worn smooth, and so on. On the whole subject of dotted letters see the well-founded criticism voiced by W. K. Pritchett in the *American Journal of Archaeology (AJA)* LIX (1955), 55–61 (*SEG* XIV 895). It is worth remarking that these dots are typographically awkward to insert, and may disappear in the course of printing. Unless cast in one piece with the letter below which they stand, they must be set in separately, and the centrifugal force of the rotary printing process may cause them to fly out of place. Their omission where they should be included may thus not necessarily be due to a lapse on the editor's part.

⁸ An attempt was made by P. Friedländer and H. B. Hoffleit in their volume *Epigrammata* (1948) to indicate more hazardous restorations, or restorations *exempli gratia*, by the use of a smaller fount, but this does not seem to have been followed up by any other author. See G. Klaffenbach, *Griechische Epigraphik*, 102 n.

CHAPTER II

¹ The decipherment of that Minoan and Mycenaean syllabic writing hitherto labelled 'Linear B' has evoked and will continue to evoke much discussion and argument, with a literature growing so fast that any attempt at a bibliography would be out of place here. The basic references consist of the first publication of Ventris' theory by himself and John Chadwick in the *Journal of Hellenic Studies* (*JHS*), LXXIII (1953), 84–103, and the same authors' definitive publication, *Documents in Mycenaean Greek* (Cambridge, 1956). For a criticism of the Ventris decipherment see A. J. Beattie in *JHS* LXXVI (1956), 1–17, with Chadwick's reply *ib.* LXXVII (1957), 202–4. Sterling Dow gave an extended history and bibliography of the discussion to date in *AJA* LVIII (1954), 77–129. See also G. Klaffenbach, *Griechische Epigraphik* (1957), 28–31.

² That it was not exclusively a 'palace art' was shown by A. J. B. Wace's discovery of tablets in a house below the citadel at Mycenae. Cf. the *Annual of the British School of Archaeology at Athens* (*BSA*), L (1955), 189. But the connexions between palace and houses may have been close, and reading and writing were techniques probably confined to people of particular *métiers*.

³ As samples of the views of the ancients themselves see Herodotus V, 58–61, Diodorus Siculus III, 67, V, 74, Tacitus, *Annals* XI, 14. Further references may be found in the handbooks; see notably F. Lenormant in Daremberg–Saglio, *Dictionnaire des Antiquités s.v.* Alphabetum, and E. Szanto in Pauly–Wissowa, *Real-Encyclopädie der classischen Altertumswissenschaft* (*R.E.*), *s.v.* Alphabet. A dissentient voice, whose opinion more closely coincides with that of much modern scholarship, is that of Josephus, *Contra Apionem*, I 10.
For the use of the word Φοινικήϊα to mean 'writing', see, apart from Herodotus, *loc. cit.*, M. N. Tod, *GHI* I² 23.

⁴ The controversy was particularly lively in the nineteen-thirties. See Rhys Carpenter, *AJA* XXXVII (1933), 8–29; *ib.* XLII (1938), 58–69; B. L. Ullman, *ib.* XXXVIII (1934), 359–81. See also Klaffenbach, *Griechische Epigraphik*, 32–5.

⁵ On what follows regarding the origin and diffusion of the Greek alphabets see the article by R. M. Cook and A. G. Woodhead to be published in *AJA* LXIII (1959), with bibliography. The epichoric inscriptions form the subject of a special and extended study by L. H. Jeffery, *The Local Scripts of Archaic Greece*. See also Klaffenbach, *Griechische Epigraphik*, 35–41, with bibliography; W. Larfeld, *Griechische Epigraphik*, §§ 145–73.

⁶ See Herodotus I, 139: τώυτὸ γράμμα, τὸ Δωριέες μὲν σὰν καλέουσι, Ἴωνες δὲ σίγμα.

⁷ The classification into 'Eastern', 'Western', and 'Southern' groups, that usually adopted, is derived from the study of A. Kirchhoff, *Studien zur*

Geschichte des griechischen Alphabets (ed. 4, 1887). Kirchhoff's map coloured the relevant areas blue, red, and green respectively, and these colour-terms are sometimes used as references to the type of alphabet they represent on the map.

[8] See example 28 at the end of Chapter IV, *SEG* XII 480.

[9] M. N. Tod, *GHI* I² 4, with bibliography. See now A. Bernand and O. Masson, *Revue des études grecques* (*REG*) LXX (1957), 1–20.

[10] See A. Schmitt, *Der Buchstabe* H *im Griechischen* (1952). A Rhodian example of the double use of H is *IG* XII 1,737.

[11] The evidence for Archinus' decree is derived from the fourth-century historian Theopompus (F. Jacoby, *Fragmente der griechischen Historiker* n. 115 frag. 155). For Ionic characters in inscriptions set up by private individuals at an earlier period see *IG* I² 588 and 618, and for Ionic intrusions into official Athenian documents see *IG* I² 18 (*SEG* X 8, XIV 2) of *c.* 457–445 B.C. and *IG* I² 39 of 446–445. *IG* I² 16 and 17 are fully Ionic texts of *c.* 465 and 445 respectively, but were inscribed at the expense of Ionic-writing cities of the Athenian empire. Texts in Ionic characters inscribed by the Athenians themselves are *SEG* X 67, 73 and 83, all of the Archidamian War, and *IG* I² 93, of the period of the Peace of Nicias. Plate 2 shows one among a number of examples of the last decade of the century.

Mr R. M. Cook advises me that in the mid-nineteenth century the dating of Attic red-figured pottery was kept too low in the mistaken belief that the Ionic lettering of inscriptions painted on it could not antedate the archonship of Euclides.

[12] On *omega* and *eta* see Rhys Carpenter, *AJA* XXXVII (1933), 22–3; *American Journal of Philology* (*AJP*), LVI (1935), 291–301; R. M. Cook and A. G. Woodhead, *BSA* XLVII (1952), 163–4.

[13] See the study of L. H. Jeffery referred to in note 5.

[14] *IG* XII 3,1075; *SEG* XIV 523.

[15] One of these is well reproduced in the photograph which forms the frontispiece to *Epigrammata*, by P. Friedländer and H. B. Hoffleit (Univ. of California, 1948).

[16] *IG* I² 761. See the comprehensive and somewhat daunting bibliographies amassed in *SEG* X 318 and XII 56.

CHAPTER III

[1] On the subject of this chapter see also W. Larfeld, *Griechische Epigraphik*, §§ 114–16; G. Klaffenbach, *Griechische Epigraphik*, 47–9.

[2] The Dipylon jug: *IG* I² 919; H. Roehl, *Imagines Inscriptionum Graecarum antiquissimarum* (ed. 3, 1907, cited hereafter as *IIG*), 69 n. 1; J. Kirchner, *Imagines Inscriptionum Atticarum* (ed. 2, 1948, cited as *IIA*), pl. 1 n.1.

The lekythos of Tataie: *IG* XIV 865; Roehl, *IIG* 79 n. 23.

The Ischia cup: *SEG* XIV 604.

[3] The Hymettus sherds: C. Blegen, *AJA* XXXVIII (1934), 10–28. Two are illustrated in Kirchner, *IIA* pl. 1 nn. 2–3.

The Mantiklos Apollo: F. R. Grace, *Archaic Sculpture in Boeotia* (1939), 49–50 and fig. 65.

[4] The Aegina plaque: *SEG* XIV 297.

[5] The Perachora curbs: H. T. Wade-Gery *ap.* H. G. G. Payne, *Perachora* (1940), 256–67; *SEG* XI 223.

Dolion's *kylichne*: *SEG* XII 480, and pp. 17 and 51 above.

[6] Around the vase: for example, *SEG* XIV 303, a Corinthian *aryballos*; around a statuette: Roehl, *IIG* 26 n. 23, *British Museum Inscriptions* n. 230, a small bronze hare from Samos now in London; on the upper surface of a statue base: M. N. Tod, *GHI* I² 3, the bases of the archaic statues of Cleobis and Biton, from Delphi.

[7] Snake-writing. See E. Zinn, *Archäologischer Anzeiger* 1950/1, 1–36.

[8] The dedication of Nicandra: Roehl, *IIG* 65 n. 2; *Inscriptions de Délos* 2.

[9] The Miletus calendar: F. Sokolowski, *Lois sacrées de l'Asie Mineure* (1955), 113–14 n. 41; *SEG* XV 673. Cf. Sokolowski, *op. cit.* nn. 42–3; *SEG* XV 674–5.

The Agora cult regulations: *SEG* XII 2–3.

The Thera column: *IG* XII 3,450; *IG* XII Suppl. p. 87.

On the dating of the late *boustrophedon* style see L. H. Jeffery, *Hesperia* XVII (1948), 103–4.

[10] The Gortyn Code: *Inscriptiones Creticae* IV, 123–71 n. 72; Roehl, *IIG* 9–12 n. 4. O. Kern, *Inscriptiones Graecae* pl. 5 (lower), gives a photograph of one section.

[11] See *SEG* XIV 391, XV 751.

[12] A striking example occurs in *IG* I² 4 (Kern, *Inscr. Graec.* pl. 13 (upper); Kirchner, *IIA* pl. 10 n. 20).

[13] *The Stoichedon Style in Greek Inscriptions* (1938). See also R. Harder, *Rottenschrift*, in *Jahrbuch des Deutschen Deutschen Archäologischen Instituts* (*Jahrb.* or *JDAI*) LVIII (1943), 93–132.

[14] E.g. *IG* I² 976 (Roehl, *IGA* p. 70 n. 3), illustrated by Austin, *op. cit.* 18.

[15] Aeakes: M. N. Tod, *GHI* I² 7; Austin, *op. cit.* 13–14.

[16] *Inscriptiones Graecae ad res Romanas pertinentes* (*IGRR*), III, 500.

[17] The incision of guide-lines is a rarity in Attica, and there is no more than a handful of examples. *IG* II² 945 and Agora I 6367 (*Hesperia* XXVI (1957), 47–51 n. 7) appear to be products of the same workshop. S. Dow, *Prytaneis*, n. 61 belongs to the same period (*c.* 180–160 B.C.). Outside Attica the practice is less uncommon, and among random instances may be cited (from Delphi) *Fouilles de Delphes* III iii, n. 383 (plate 4), J. Bousquet, *BCH* LXXX (1956), 564, fig. 8 (cf. 580 note 1) and pl. X; (from Camirus) M. Segre—I.

Pugliese Carratelli, *Annuario della Scuola Italiana archeologica di Atene* n.s. XI–XIII (1949–51), 143–4 n. 1, 183 n. 25, and others; (from Thera) Kern, *Inscr. Graec.* pl. 33 (upper).

This type of guide-line differs from those horizontal lines used also for decorative effect, which form an integral part of the inscription, such as those illustrated in fig. 2 and occurring, for example, in *Hesperia* VIII (1939), 166 (*SEG* XI 305).

[18] An Athenian decree of 450–449 B.C. regulating the affairs of Miletus. See B. D. Meritt, H. T. Wade-Gery, and M. F. McGregor, *The Athenian Tribute Lists* II, D 11; *SEG* X 14, XIV 4.

CHAPTER IV

[1] On this chapter see also W. Larfeld, *Griechische Epigraphik*, §§ 196–308; G. Klaffenbach, *Griechische Epigraphik*, 50–89. Klaffenbach devotes to a discussion of the various kinds of inscriptions his longest and fullest section.

[2] In *Inscriptiones Graecae* (*IG*) II^2 the final volume, containing nos. 5220–13247, includes the *tituli sepulcrales*, among which the *monumenta privata* (5228–13187) are arranged in the following order:

   i. Names with demotics. The demes are dealt with in alphabetical order, and within each deme the arrangement is in order of the first letter of the name of the deceased.

   ii. Names with ethnics. The division is, first, by cities and countries in order of the first letter of their name, and in alphabetical order of the deceased within each group.

   iii. Names without either demotic or ethnic. A list in alphabetical order.

   iv. Fragments where not even the name of the deceased survives (these are mainly verse epitaphs).

   A further section (13188–13228) lists those epitaphs which invoke a penalty or curse on any person disturbing the tomb.

[3] Collected in *IG* IV^2 1.

[4] Examples illustrating some of the categories referred to in the following sections are collected at the end of the chapter. Plates 1–3 further give examples of transactions of the βουλή and δῆμος, and show prescripts of the fifth (pls. 1–2) and later fourth (pl. 3) centuries.

[5] The full record of amendments was discontinued in Attica from 275 B.C. or so onwards: outside Attica they are unusual in any case. I note with interest that this same example (*IG* I^2 118) is that selected by Klaffenbach for a similar purpose (*op. cit.* 70); it is useful from a variety of points of view. For amendments to amendments see *IG* I^2 39.

[6] See *The Erechtheum* (1927), ed. J. M. Paton. The inscriptions, edited by L. D. Caskey, are to be found on pp. 277–422.

[7] *Dedications from the Athenian Akropolis* (1949).

NOTES TO CHAPTER IV

⁸ See W. Peek, *Griechische Vers-Inschriften* I, for the complete collection
to 1955, and the review by the present author in the *Classical Review (Cl.
Rev.*), n.s. VII (1957), pp. 115–18.

⁹ See M. N. Tod, *BSA* XLVI (1951), 182–90.

¹⁰ G. Klaffenbach has dealt at greater length with manumissions on pp. 83–8
of *Griechische Epigraphik*. It is worth noting that in some types of manumission the slave was 'bought' by the god or by some private person, with a
view to his freedom and on his promise to refund the purchase money.

CHAPTER V

¹ On this section see also G. Klaffenbach, *Griechische Epigraphik*, 93–6.

² The date of Stratonicea. It is disputed whether this foundation is to be
attributed to Antiochus I or Antiochus II of Syria. For a recent note on the
subject see J. and L. Robert, *Mélanges Isidore Lévy* (1955), 567.

³ *Inschriften von Olympia* 266, 630, and 631.

⁴ See especially L. Robert, *Études Anatoliennes* (1937), 433, *Hellenica* X
(1955), 94; J. M. R. Cormack, *History of the Inscribed Monuments of Aphro-
disias* (1955), 3. On the Leiden inscriptions see H. W. Pleket, *The Greek
Inscriptions in the 'Rijksmuseum van Oudheden' at Leyden* (1958).

⁵ Cf. L. Robert, *Hellenica* X, 134–50 and elsewhere.

⁶ Now in the British Museum, a gift of King George IV. See M. N. Tod,
Greek Historical Inscriptions I² 22.

⁷ M. N. Tod, *Greek Historical Inscriptions* II 187.

⁸ Above, pp. 46–7.

⁹ On the character and problems of the Athenian calendar see Chapter X
below, pp. 115–18.

¹⁰ E.g. *IG* II² 967, of 145/4 B.C., lines 3–5. Ἐλαφηβολιῶνο[ς] | ἐνάτει
μετ' εἰκάδας κατ' ἄρχοντα, κατὰ θεὸν [δ]ὲ [Μ]ουνιχιῶνος δωδε[κά]||τει.

¹¹ See V. Ehrenberg and A. H. M. Jones, *Documents illustrating the reigns
of Augustus and Tiberius* (ed. 2, 1955), 98.

¹² See Margaret Crosby, *Hesperia* XIX (1950), 189–312, XXVI (1957),
1–23; R. J. Hopper, *BSA* XLVIII (1953), 200–54.

¹³ See O. W. Reinmuth, *Hesperia* XXIV (1955), 225–8.

¹⁴ On laudatory epithets in funerary inscriptions see M. N. Tod, *BSA*
XLVI (1951), 182–90.

¹⁵ Nor is it even uniform at the same time in the same place. Compare, for
example, the very different forms of two identical dedications illustrated in
the *Journal of Egyptian Archaeology (JEA)*, XXXVIII (1952), plate XIV.

¹⁶ Some of the features are visible on the squeeze of an inscription of the
third century A.D., from Asia Minor, illustrated in plate 4.

[17] *IG* II^2 2679. See J. V. A. Fine, *Horoi* (*Hesperia* Suppl. IX, 1951), 49–50. They occur sporadically from the third century onwards. For examples derived from Lesbian inscriptions, and their value as evidence for the cursive script of the time, see J. Boüüaert, *La Nouvelle Clio* VI (1954), 354–77, criticised by L. Robert, *Comptes-rendus de l'Académie des Inscriptions et Belles-lettres* (*CRAI*) (1955), 195–219.

CHAPTER VI

[1] For the attempt made at such a distinction by P. Friedländer and H. B. Hoffleit see Chapter I note 8. See also the pertinent remarks of G. Klaffenbach, *Griechische Epigraphik*, 100–1, who quotes a long pronouncement by L. Robert (*Hellenica* I (1940), 149–50) on the same subject.

[2] See B. D. Meritt, *Epigraphica Attica* (1940), 129. The doctrine of this book underlies much of the present chapter.

[3] An interesting example of this is offered by a new fragment of Agora I. 994 (see E. Schweigert, *Hesperia* IX (1940), 314–20 n. 31), an Athenian statue-base connected with the war of 377–374 B.C. The new piece belongs to the left side of the left face of this base, displacing fragment *A* which Schweigert had located there. Fragment *A* might, on the evidence of the squeezes, be fitted in either further to the right on this same face, or at the left end of the main (front) face. A test with the stones, however, reveals that the configuration of the fragments below the surface makes the adoption of either solution impossible. In order to accommodate this fragment, the base must be presumed to have been larger than Schweigert thought it was.

[4] See the references given in *SEG* XIII 1.

[5] See B. D. Meritt, *Epigraphica Attica*, 80–2.

[6] A method applied with conspicuous success, for example, by O. W. Reinmuth in his reconstruction (*Hesperia* XXIV (1955), 220–39; *SEG* XV 104) of a long ephebic inscription composed of some thirty-five fragments.

[7] *Epigraphica Attica*, 49–53.

[8] See the drawing in *Epigraphica Attica*, 77, fig. 16.

[9] *Epigraphica Attica*, 79–80.

[10] *Epigraphica Attica*, 82–3.

[11] Chapter III, p. 32.

[12] The value of these formulas for dating purposes has already been discussed in the previous chapter (p. 61).

[13] *SEG* XII 242, from Delphi, of the first century B.C.

['Αρχ]οντος 'Η[ρα]κλείδα τοῦ Εὐκλείδα, μηνὸς [----, βουλευόντων Φιλο νίκου, 'Αθανίων]ος, Στράτωνος, 'Εμμε- νίδα, ἐπὶ τοῖσδε ἀπέδοτο Εὐάγγελος Μεγάρτα, [συνευδοκέοντος καὶ τοῦ υἱοῦ Μεγάρ]τα, τῶι 'Απόλλωνι τῶι Πυ- θίωι σῶμα ἀνδρεῖον ὧι ὄνομα Σώσιππος, [τιμᾶς ἀργυρίου μνᾶν ----], καὶ τὰν τιμὰν ἔχει πᾶσαν,

καθὼς ἐπίστευσε Σώσιππος τῶι θεῶι τὰν [ὠνάν, ἐφ' ὧιτε ἐλεύθερος εἶμεν
καὶ ἀνέφα]πτος [ἀ]πὸ πάντων τὸν πάν-
5 τα βίον· βεβαιωτὴρ Λαιάδας Ἄγωνος· εἰ δέ [τις ἐφάπτοιτο Σωσίππου ἐπὶ
καταδουλ]ισμῶι, βέβαιον παρεχόντω
τῶι θεῶι τὰν ὠνὰν ὅ τε ἀποδόμενος καὶ ὁ βε[βαιωτήρ· ὁμοίως δὲ καὶ ὁ
παρατυχὼν κ]ύριος ἔστω συλέων ἀζάμι-
ος ὢν καὶ ἀνυπόδικος πάσας δίκας καὶ ζαμίας. [Μάρτυροι οἵ τε ἱερεῖς τοῦ
Ἀπόλλ]ωνος Αἰακίδας, Ξενοκράτης, καὶ ἰδι-
ῶται Καλλίδαμος, Πύρρος, Σώτας.

¹⁴ A proxeny decree of 429/8 or 421/0 B.C.

[Ἔδοχσεν τει βολ]ε̄ι κ[αὶ το̄ι δέμο]-   Στοιχ. 25.
[ι· .ι. εἶς ἐπρυτ]άνευ[ε, ᶜ·⁵.... ἐπε]-
[στάτε, ...ᶜ·⁷...]ς ἐγρα[μμάτευε, .]
[....⁸.... ἔρχε, Ε]ὔφεμ[ος εἶπε· κα]-
5 [λέσαι μὲν ..⁵..]αῖον [τὸν ..⁵..]
[... ἐπὶ χσένια ἐ]ς τὸ πρ[υτανεῖο]-
[ν καὶ ἐπαινέσαι h]ότι ν[ῦν τε ἀνὲ]-
[ρ ἀγαθός ἐστι περ]ὶ Ἀθε[ναίος κα]-
[ὶ ἐν τῶι πρόσθεν χρόνοι· ἔναι δὲ]
10 [αὐτὸν καὶ τὸς παῖδας προχσένο]-
[ς καὶ εὐεργέτας Ἀθεναίον καὶ π]-
[ρόσοδον ἔναι αὐτοῖς πρὸς τὲν β]-
[ολὲν καὶ τὸν δῆμον ὁς εὐεργέτα]-
[ις ὅσιν Ἀθεναίον πρό]τ[οι]σι [μεθ']
15 [hιερά· προσαγόντον] δὲ [οἱ] π[ρυτά]-
[νες οἳ ἂν ἀεὶ ὄ[σι· καὶ ὁς [ἂ]ν μὲ [ἀδι]-
[κε̄ται τούτ]ον [με]δ[έ]ς, hοι στρατε-
[γοὶ hοὶ] ἂν ὅσι [hεκά]στο[τ]ε καὶ hε
[βολὲ h]ε βολεύο[σ]α καὶ hοι πρυτά-
20 [νες ἑκά]στοτε ἐ[πι]μελέσθον αὐ[τ]-
[ον· τὸ δὲ φ]σέφισ[μα] τόδε ἀνα[γραφ]-
[σάτο hο γρ]αμμα[τε]ὺς hο [τε̄ς βολε̄]-
[ς ἐν στέλει] λιθ[ίν]ει [καὶ καταθέ]-
[το ἐμ πόλει]· ἔνα[ι δὲ καὶ εὐεργεσ]-
25 [ίαν καὶ προ]χσε[νίαν αὐτοῖς καὶ]
[ἐκγόνοις(?) ------------------]

¹⁵ BCH LII (1928), 174–6.

¹⁶ M. F. McGregor, in his review of A. E. Raubitschek's *Dedications from the Athenian Akropolis* (*Classical Philology* XLVII (1952), 32–5), put on record wise and clear advice which is worth quoting. 'The epigraphist today deals with the most vital and perhaps the only new evidence that is likely to be granted to the historian. He must therefore exercise the most scrupulous caution. He must never feel embarrassment when he leaves a text without

restoration; and he must specify clearly when his supplements are printed by way of example.' Relegation of such *exempli gratia* restorations to a footnote or to the commentary rather than their inclusion in the main text is certainly the safer course and offers less chance of a misunderstanding.

CHAPTER VII

[1] See B. D. Meritt, *Epigraphica Attica*, 20–2. In reading a badly weathered, battered, or defaced text, as Meritt says, 'one must use every device at his disposal' for recovering the correct reading. This seems, therefore, a suitable point at which to mention the use of a mixture of charcoal and water which, spread lightly about on the stone with the fingers, runs into the cuts and crevices and helps to pick out, on an almost smooth surface, such traces of letters as there may be, often not otherwise visible to the eye.

The accurate measurement of the stone must in any case be carried out on the spot, whether or no a drawing is also made. The measurement (in metres) should record the maximum width, height and thickness of the stone, the height of the letters, and the *stoichedon* intervals (if applicable).

[2] The paper used at the Museum of Classical Archaeology, Cambridge, is a no. 3 grade filter paper, supplied by Messrs A. Gallenkamp and Sons of London. The American epigraphists prefer a thinner paper, squeeze paper no. 21 of 10 lb. weight, supplied by Messrs Carter, Rice, Storrs, and Bement of Boston, Mass.

To help stored squeezes to withstand handling and the general effect of age, they may be sprayed with a solution of methyl methacrylate resin (4 per cent in acetone and ethylene dichloride). Such a solution is manufactured by the Rohm and Haas Company of Philadelphia and sold under the trade name of Acryloid B-7. See Earl R. Caley and B. D. Meritt, *Journal of Documentary Reproduction* III (1940), 204–5.

[3] For another description of squeeze-making see R. Bloch, *L'épigraphie latine* (1952), 12–13.

[4] It may be mentioned that the leisurely taking of squeezes in a museum, with all the necessary equipment to hand in quiet surroundings, is a vastly different matter from the often hurried work in the field, with wind and dust blowing or rain falling, which sometimes falls to the epigraphist's lot. See *Epigraphica Attica*, 42. Most epigraphists have had bitter and frustrating experiences of this sort, and a history of trial and tribulation lies behind many an innocent-looking squeeze.

In the process of drying squeezes shrink slightly and distort, according to the type and quality of the paper used (cf. *Epigraphica Attica*, 41–2). Such distortion should always be borne in mind in working from squeezes, and especially in making measurements or comparisons from them.

[5] See *AJA* LVI (1952), 118–20; LVII (1953), 197–8.

⁶ However, successful squeezes of vertical faces have been taken, and large areas have been squeezed with notable success. Squeezes made at Nimrûd have been particularly good examples of the use of liquid rubber, and there is no doubt that the difficulties mentioned in the text will be overcome with further testing and experience.

⁷ See *Epigraphica Attica*, 24–41; J. J. E. Hondius, *Saxa Loquuntur* (1938), 2–3.

⁸ As a useful device for improvising reflectors to catch what light there is, the traveller can do worse than to take with him a roll of aluminium foil, as sold in grocery stores for cooking or wrapping purposes. Strips of this may be torn off to the required size and may help immeasurably in improving the conditions under which a photograph can be taken. If nothing else is available, clean sheets of white squeeze paper, strategically placed, will do much to improve the quality of the lighting.

⁹ M. B. Cookson, *Photography for Archaeologists* (1954). Cf. R. J. C. Atkinson, *Field Archaeology* (1946), 156–64; Sir Mortimer Wheeler, *Archaeology from the Earth* (1954), 174–81.

CHAPTER VIII

¹ For artists' signatures see E. Loewy, *Inschriften griechischer Bildhauer* (Leipzig, 1885); J. Marcadé, *Recueil des signatures de sculpteurs grecs* (1953–). Works on grave-reliefs, such as H. Diepolder, *Die attischen Grabreliefs des 5. und 4. Jahrhunderts v. Chr.* (1931), or Alice Muehsam, *Attic grave reliefs from the Roman period* (in *Berytus* X (1952), 51–114), illustrate the inscriptions together with the sculpture they accompany.

² R. Binneboessel, *Studien zu den attischen Urkundenreliefs des 5. und 4. Jahrhunderts* (1932).

³ There is a good series of photographs of inscriptions from Egypt in E. Breccia, *Iscrizioni greche e latine* (*Catalogue général des antiquités égyptiennes du Musée d'Alexandrie*, 1911).

CHAPTER IX

¹ No attempt is made here to give any kind of history of epigraphic studies, which is in itself a fascinating and rewarding subject. G. Klaffenbach treats the matter of this chapter, with a little more detail on the historical aspects, in *Griechische Epigraphik*, 12–20. For a full and comprehensive account down to 1914 see W. Larfeld, *Griechische Epigraphik*, §§ 3–100. Cf. also S. Chabert, *Histoire sommaire des études d'épigraphie grecque* (1906).

² Le Bas seems to have been the first to take squeezes on any extensive scale in the course of his epigraphical journeys. He was not, however, the first to make use of them at all, as was suggested by Hondius (*Saxa Loquuntur*, 16). Pighius is on record as having used them, and in his life of the seventeenth-

century scholar Raffaele Fabretti (*Vitae Italorum doctrina excellentium qui saeculo XVII floruerunt*, Rome 1770, decas III, pp. 194–5) Angelo Fabroni describes the use and making of paper squeezes.

3 It remains arguable that, in such cases as these, the texts should be edited separately and kept distinct from the general work for which they form the principal evidence. Embedded within a larger dissertation, they are less readily located and appreciated in comparative study with material from the same area, which the *corpus*-arrangement makes most easy. References to material published in such works for the first time are also more complicated, unless it is also reproduced in *SEG* or some similar work and so given the simple reference of a volume and number.

4 *TAM* III, fasc. 1, contains the inscriptions of the city of Termessus in Pisidia.

5 On the *Sammelbuch* see the pertinent remarks of P. M. Fraser in *JEA* XXXVIII (1952), 115–18 no. 8.

CHAPTER X

1 M. N. Tod, *BSA* XVIII (1911–12), 98–132; XXVIII (1926–7), 141–57; XXXVII (1936–7), 236–57; XLV (1950), 126–39. See also *JHS* XXXIII (1913), 27–34. Cf. *Companion to Greek Studies* (ed. 4, 1931), 698–9; W. Larfeld, *Griechische Epigraphik*, §§ 184–92.

2 Note that the Roman subtraction-method (e.g. X minus I for 9, with the lower figure written *before* the higher—IX) is not used in Greek; it is uncommon even in Latin epigraphy.

3 Herodian (Aelius Herodianus, second cent. A.D.), Περὶ τῶν ἀριθμῶν. See the appendix to vol. VIII of the Didot edition of Stephanus, *Thesaurus Linguae Graecae*, p. 345.

4 M. N. Tod, *BSA* XLV (1950), 129.

5 For 'letter-labels' see M. N. Tod, *BSA* XLIX (1954), 1–8.

6 See M. N. Tod, *Greek Historical Inscriptions* I² 24. An isolated instance of alphabetic numerals apparently used as such in the fifth century occurs in *IG* I² 760.

7 W. S. Ferguson, *The Athenian Secretaries* (1898), *Athenian Tribal Cycles in the Hellenistic Age* (1932).

8 The first two or three letters of each name may be combined into a mnemonic, which some people find helpful:

ERAIPALEAK – OIKEHIPPAIANT.

9 On the date see W. K. Pritchett, *The five Attic tribes after Kleisthenes* (1943), 13–23.

[10] See A. H. McDonald and F. W. Walbank, *JRS* XXVII (1937), 180–207; F. W. Walbank, *Philip V of Macedon* (1940), 129–32; W. K. Pritchett, *Transactions of the American Philological Association* LXXXV (1954), 159–67 (especially 162–4).

[11] The work cited above in note 9.

[12] In his article cited in note 10.

[13] See for this section W. K. Pritchett and O. Neugebauer, *The Calendars of Athens* (1947), and various works by B. D. Meritt (e.g. *The Athenian Calendar in the Fifth Century* (1928) and *Athenian Financial Documents* (1932), 152–79) and W. B. Dinsmoor (e.g. *The Archons of Athens in the Hellenistic Age* (1931)).

[14] Note that *popularly*, i.e. in ordinary parlance, the lunar calendar would always be used.

[15] For the machine used in this process see Sterling Dow, *Prytaneis* (*Hesperia* Supplement I, 1937), 198–215.

[16] Here again a mnemonic may prove useful:
Hek-Met-Bo : Py-Mai-Po : Gam-Anth-El : Moun-Thar-Skir.

[17] See also W. Larfeld, *Handbuch der Griechischen Epigraphik* I (1907), 301–2. For recent examples of amendments to knowledge of local calendars see M. Guarducci, *Annuario* n.s. III–V (1941–3), 145–7, on the month Ἀγυῆος and the calendar of Argos, G. Daux, *BCH* LXXX (1956), 433–5, on the month Δάτυιος in Epirus, and P. Charneux, *BCH* LXXXI (1957), 197–202, on the order of months at Argos and Epidaurus.

INDEX